ILLUMINATION:
Joseph's Vision

This book is dedicated to Tony
at the Sanctuary of Healing,
whose generosity made its publication possible.

www.thesanctuaryofhealing.co.uk

ILLUMINATION:
Joseph's Vision

channelled by Michael G. Reccia

with essential contributions from:
Jane Kneen • David Openshaw

Copyright © Band of Light Media Limited 2009

Published by Band of Light Media Limited

c/o The Sanctuary of Healing,
Dewhurst Road,
Langho, Blackburn,
Lancashire, BB6 8AF

ISBN: 978-1-906625-01-6

First Edition November 2009

Printed in Great Britain by the MPG Books Group, Bodmin and King's Lynn

Contents

An introduction by Michael 9

The Field and The Fall – a brief explanation 13

1: The cyclic nature of you and the universe 15

2: You are dreaming reality 24

3: You change 'The Field' through joy 34

4: Tear down your walls! 48

5: Be careful what you ask for 61

6: Neutralising your fears and temptations 72

7: You possess the ultimate super-weapon 83

8: You can work magic in your life 93

9: Questioning your approach to religion 99

10: Freeing yourself from oppressive tendencies 112

11: Finding your peace within 123

12: You are here today – you are gone tomorrow . . . 134

13: Are you moving or standing still? 144

14: How to stop 'The Field' slowing you down 152

15: You change the world 167

Index 178

ILLUMINATION

An introduction by Michael

What on Earth do you do when, after years of working as a medium in the 'accepted' way (i.e: that of bringing through information from deceased family members to provide evidence of life after death to their relatives on Earth) you suddenly begin to receive communications from a highly evolved spirit guide called *Joseph* that delve into and explain the human condition from the point of view of 'spiritual physics' in intricate detail – life-changing, powerful, *amazing* information to challenge the way we look at life, death, Creation, the power of our minds and hearts and our purpose in being here?

What on Earth do you do when communications are received that concisely, precisely and in a spiritual but completely non-religious way embrace every single soul on this planet and satisfyingly answer the age-old questions every human being must surely ask at some stage in their existence – questions such as: 'Who am I?', 'What am I?', 'Why am I here?', 'Where am I going?', 'Is this all there is?' and 'What am I really capable of?'

What on Earth you do is the only thing you possibly *can* do in good conscience – hold regular contact sessions to bring through the communications from *Joseph* then painstakingly gather them into book form (as he requested us to do) and release it so that the information it contains can be made available to those who truly want to understand and change their lives for the better – so that's precisely what I and my colleagues in the *Band of Light* (the organisation named for us by *Joseph* and tasked with bringing through his communications and the work of other guiding influences) did in 2008.

Following the release of **Revelation: Joseph's Message** it quickly became apparent that *Joseph* had more than one book in him – much more, in fact, and that subsequent volumes would not be mere sequels to the original covering the same ground but, instead, could be read as stand-alone pieces that would also add to and enhance the first with entirely new information. *Joseph*'s message concerns itself, as I mentioned, with the whys and wherefores of our place here and in the universe, with what is wrong in our world and, more importantly, why efforts to redress the balance, as the centuries have passed, have led to little if any improvement in the human condition. Indeed, it would be hard not to argue that things have become considerably worse, increasingly violent and more discordant as the years have passed.

This, his second book, is a spiritual 'manual' that empowers us to make changes for the better, not just in our own lives, but also in the lives of others and in the world around us as a whole.

Unlike some spiritual communications *Joseph*'s messages are delivered with a forthright urgency and a contemporary approach to language. For example, there are no 'thees' and 'thous' and archaic or convoluted turns of phrase in this volume – logically what use would such ancient flourishes be to the twenty-first century reader, and why shouldn't an advanced soul, fully aware of how life in this century is lived, be able to communicate succinctly in a way today's audience can fully relate to?

Joseph has stated again and again that time is running out for us and our world *unless we do something about it now* and, in no uncertain terms, this book demonstrates that it is up to each of us to work spiritually to put things right, simply and firmly giving us the means to do just that through changing our personal and worldwide perspectives and by providing simple yet effective exercises to help us achieve the goals of personal and global peace, wellbeing, reconciliation, reconstruction and happiness.

Throughout the writing of this book my personal spiritual perspective was changing too... *Joseph*'s previous volume had been dictated to me 'clairaudiently' – that is, through the facility of mediumistic hearing, with me 'tuning in', listening to *Joseph*'s voice and repeating what he was saying to me into a recorder. Although the early chapters of this book were obtained by the same method, this was to be a period of transition for me as a medium, and much of this second volume would be dictated *through* me whilst I was in a trance state, with the effect that I only became aware of the information I had been used as a means of delivering once it had been transcribed.

Also during this period we (myself, of course, plus two untiring and dedicated fellow spiritual seekers and workers for the Light – my partner Jane and long-time friend and business partner David) began to take *Joseph* 'on the road' with 'An Audience With *Joseph*' – a number of trance evenings held with his permission and encouragement at which *Joseph* would take over my mind, body and vocal chords by placing me in trance then invite and answer questions from the audience.

In terms of years and dimensions travelled *Joseph* has come a long, long way to deliver his vital communications (although he would, with his characteristic sense of humour, be the first to point out that, from a spiritual perspective, no one actually goes anywhere at all!) and continues to work with us on future books. The reason he does this is because, as he says, he *cares* – both for us as individuals and also for this crippled, exploited planet which he wishes, in a very real sense, to give us the means to reinvigorate and save. In considering and practising what he suggests in this volume you prove that you care too, and you will be quietly and discretely working to make not only your own life a richer, more fulfilled experience, but creating – actually and actively *creating* – a better world for everyone else on this planet and ensuring that not only will future generations benefit too, but that there will indeed be future generations on Earth.

Thank you for choosing to read **Illumination: Joseph's Vision.**

The full story of how *Joseph* and the *Band of Light* came to work together is included in **Revelation: Joseph's Message,** and we'd be delighted if you would visit us at: www.michaelandjane.co.uk and www.josephspeaks.com for more inspired information from *Joseph* and many other guides. A free newsletter is also available, plus details of forthcoming 'Audience with *Joseph*' evenings.

Michael G. Reccia.
October, 2009.

Terminology: 'The Field', 'The Fall' – a brief explanation

If you are new to the *Joseph* Communications and have not read **Revelation: Joseph's Message**, the first book in this series, allow me to qualify the terms 'The Field' and 'The Fall', which *Joseph* often mentions in this second volume.

The Field.

When referring to 'The Field' *Joseph* is describing the conscious field of thought-energy we, as spirits on Earth, are surrounded by and live within. Every second of our lives we project our thoughts and beliefs as to the nature of reality into this energy field. The Field is actually created and maintained *by us*, but we have lost sight of this fact. As a result of us forgetting this, which is in itself as a result of 'The Fall' (see below), The Field is not operating as it was originally intended to. It was supposed to serve us, but at the moment we, in effect, serve it. It exhibits, and seeks to perpetuate in us, a negative charge and outlook, and, because of this and its disconnection with God-Light, is maintaining itself and us via a finite and dwindling amount of energy. The Field in its present state, and therefore also we as human beings existing within it, cannot last much longer. *Joseph* urges us to re-energise The Field with God-Light and, by doing so, to transform it and take control of it once again for the betterment and continuance of mankind and of the planet.

The Fall.

...is a term that *Joseph* applies to a complex decision and action taken by human souls millions of years ago which resulted in a cataclysmic change in vibration that plunged the Earth into a darkness we and the planet are still suffering from and feeling the effects of. This change in vibration separated us in conscious thought from our God-heritage and resulted in the negative, violent, power-hungry world and society we currently live in. The Fall is a vast and fascinating subject, and a book is in preparation chronicling exactly what happened at the time this event took place and the consequences of it having done so.

ILLUMINATION

Chapter 1

The cyclic nature of you and the universe

Michael's notes. As explained in the introduction to this volume *Joseph*'s second book began to unfold at a time of great spiritual transition for me personally. This first chapter was given to our little group in the usual way, in that we sat together to contact *Joseph* via the traditional mediumistic clairaudient link I had relied on to bring through his first book – **Revelation: Joseph's Message**. At the end of the month in which this chapter had been delivered, however, I was due to hold my first public demonstration of trance mediumship, having been carefully prepared in private for this new way of working for some time by certain of my guides. As I began to work openly as a trance medium the established routine of our group contacting *Joseph* through clairaudience was replaced by my regularly being taken into trance to deliver the chapters for this book, allowing *Joseph*, rather than dictating his words by overshadowing me*, to actually take over my physical and mental faculties during those times in which he wished to speak to us. This new way of communicating led to an extension of the amount of time at any one of our meetings during which I could work with *Joseph*; to an even greater amount of information coming through in each communication, and to the unfortunate after-effect of me, not strictly having been present except

---

*When overshadowing me *Joseph* moves in close to 'touch' my aura so that he can dominate the communication without actually taking me into trance.

as a physical 'shell' to host *Joseph*, having little to no recollection of what had been said on each occasion! We doubled up on our audio equipment, making absolutely sure that *Joseph*'s words were recorded on and downloaded to as many separate pieces of equipment as we could lay our hands on so that the chances of his communications being lost were virtually nil. For this first chapter, however, the link would be the tried and tested clairaudient one which, as stated, had been the means of receiving the contents of the whole of book one…

This first session begins with me passing on what *Joseph* is saying, acting at first as a repeater of his clairaudiently heard words. He then gradually takes over the communication as he overshadows me…

Michael. Where do you want to start *Joseph*?

…*Joseph* says he wants to start at the beginning – at the *very* beginning – because he promised that this second book would be about man's potential – and he wants to open the book by talking about the beginning of the universe. He says that scientists *are* correct – the universe came from nothing and it did come from an explosion – an explosion of energy, an explosion of 'reality' that began to expand, and that everything we see on this physical level is contained within that explosion. He says that the problem is we cannot see behind that physical level; we cannot see where the universe came from and we cannot, as a rule, as souls, see beyond this physical universe whilst we are here on Earth.

Joseph speaks. …Everything that happens externally is a mirror of what can happen *within* a soul and that is one of God's gifts to us. God says, 'Look at what is happening – seemingly outside of yourselves – and you will see what you are capable of *within* yourselves.'

The universe came from a point; that dot-within-the-circle. I gave you the ancient symbol of the dot-within-the-circle (see **Revelation: Joseph's Message**) for a purpose, not just to say 'here is a symbol' but to say that *everything,* as I have said before, *is contained within that circle.* So the physical universe is finite in that it is contained within that circle. It may be expanding but it is expanding as a wavelength outwards to a point where, in terms of physicality, it will reach the edges of that circle, of that sphere. Then, when it reaches the edges of the sphere, it will begin to contract and be pulled back slowly, slowly, *slowly,* to the dot in the centre of the circle. So everything in a physical universe is embraced within that circle that is God and proceeds from that dot that is also God: God is the giver, God is the container.

…And this pulse has happened before. Scientists look at the universe and some say the universe is a unique event, that it will reach a certain length and point in time and then it will cease to exist. What they don't understand is that the manifestation and re-absorption of the physical universe is a *repeating cycle*. It may seem to a soul that is *living within it* too vast and solid to be a cycle but nevertheless it is. It may take millions and millions and billions and trillions of years but it expands from that dot and it goes back to that dot. Everything goes back to that dot and then the dot is put forwards again as another expression of physicality.

So God is not only a circle (the circle has no beginning and no end. God has no beginning and no end – that is God's nature) … God is not only the dot-within-the-circle – God is *a cycle* – is cyclic in nature – too. And the knowledge that is accumulated as the universe expands is then pulled in from the circle to the dot to make each subsequent cycle even more polished, to make each cycle even more evolved, to progress each cycle. So, God *progresses* – becomes more than He is – via the cycle, the wavelength, that brings the universe out and then back in again.

Because everything is contained within God, we – who contribute to making God more than He is whilst and by living our physical lives – are also part of God. It is not that God is having to depend on human beings who are 'less than perfect' (according to religion and lore) to

17

perfect Himself; it is that God is putting out more of Himself, expanding Himself so that, within successive expansions – cycles – different concepts can be explored through the experiences of various manifestations of souls as physical beings, both human and animal in the case of the Earth, which are then taken back to the heart of God via those souls when they are freed from physical matter and return to the spiritual realms, so that the heart of God can be further refined and send out new concepts.

And that, my friends, is just the nature of the *physical* universe. There are *other* universes. There are *spiritual* universes, which are all based on the same principle: an expansion of matter, an expansion of energy, to allow form to take place, and an expansion of thought and concept and understanding within that form that then is withdrawn to the centre to be put out again in ever more refined form.

And you might ask, 'Well, Joseph, is there anything *outside* of God?' I can only answer from within my experience, and all that I have come across in all my experiences, and all that anyone that I have ever met or linked with from 'higher' or 'lower' spheres of existence has experienced, has been contained within the will of God, within the creative faculty of God, within the senses of God, the vibrations of God. My *heart mind* answer (which is based not on the factual knowledge assimilated by the head mind you use on Earth but on soul-core understanding, knowing and perception) is therefore: 'No, there is nothing outside of God. *There is nothing outside of God*; God contains everything.'

A question also sometimes asked is: 'Is there more than one God?' Again, my answer to that (based on my personal experience) is: 'No, everything is contained within the *Oneness* – there can only be Oneness.' No matter how evolved, how enlightened a spirit may become they are still part of the Oneness; they do not become a *separate* God. They display more God-Energy, they have a greater understanding of God, but they are still part of God. So, my answer is that *everything is contained within* the one *God but also that God is contained within everything – within **everything**.*

My point in opening this second book in this way is to say to the people who will read it, to the people who will listen to it (because it will also be made available in different forms – including a form that you can listen to): God is '*without*' you – He is outside of you and around you, containing you, protecting you, but He is also '*inside*' you.

That universe that expands from the dot to the edges of the cycle and then goes back again is also within you and, if you think about it, this is also the way in which you operate as a soul on Earth, as a physical being. The point of birth is the explosion of physicality from that dot, from the soul that you really are. You then reach the outer limits of understanding within a lifetime in a physical universe and then you pass on (you 'die', as you say), you move on to another area of existence and that knowledge is condensed within you so that your soul, when you go back to the spirit worlds, can take advantage of it. And then there is a new existence for you where the dot is put forth again, perhaps in physicality, perhaps in another realm in the spirit worlds, but that cycle of journeying outwards and then coming back into the centre – growing outwards and then coming into the centre – is reflected in all things, including yourself.

The object of this book is to make you aware of your potential as a soul but also to make you aware of your potential, your capability, as a *human being* – because, as a human being, you contain within you all the building blocks you need to create whatever you want to create: to build a different society, to heal society, to heal yourself, to bring yourself to new frontiers of knowledge, to change the face of this Earth, to reach outwards towards other planets if you so wish to do as a race. *All that potential is contained within you.*

Unfortunately that potential is not being realised at this time because people are being given no true spiritual encouragement. People have lost their way and are lost in the '*illusion*' of the world. They are lost in what they see outside themselves, not realising that what they see outside themselves is created from inside themselves. It is no use railing against society and saying it is wrong. You, all of you *en masse*, have created society as it is. True, the souls who came before you contributed to it but 'reality' is like a switch – it can be switched on and off at will.

My message to you, which we will investigate in future chapters, in future words, is that it is no use complaining about society if you are not prepared to switch that switch. It is no use saying, 'What can I do?' It is no use saying, 'I'm not bothered, I'm safe.' You have to take the view that it is up to you. *Each person has to take the view that it is up to them to change things.* If you believe it is up to the politicians you are wrong. If you believe it is up to the clergyman you are wrong. If you believe it is up to local councils, or police, or solicitors, or judges you are wrong!

Society changes with you.

There is an expression: *the buck stops here.* The buck stops with you! You, as part of God, are all powerful. You, as part of God, are all goodness. You, as part of God, are all Love. It is only because you have forgotten these things that you do not manifest them in your society at the moment.

You will be aware that the first book that has been published introduces me as an Atlantean... and, yes, that is one of the lives I lived on Earth that I am most comfortable with. I wish I could take you back to that time. I wish I could show you the splendour, the beauty of the world as it was at that time. I wish you could see the bronzed trees under purple skies. I wish you could see the art we created with gold that was beaten out so fine it was almost transparent. I wish you could see the fruits that we grew. I wish you could see the communities we had. ...And we lost it all because of man sinking into his own illusion.

I have returned to Earth as the spokesperson of a number of souls to make sure that the mistakes that were made around the time of Atlantis are not made again. That idyll, that beauty we had, can be yours again. Not as something to be coveted by the few but as something to be enjoyed by all souls on Earth, to thank God for. That perfection, that symmetry you do not see presently can be yours again. It starts with you. It starts today. It starts now. It starts the minute you read this. There is no time to waste!

In subsequent chapters I am going to tell you how you can change society and *you change society first of all by changing yourself.* This book is about new visions; this book is about giving yourself the ability to dream again; this book is about projecting into the ether the society you want – that God wants – and *this book, ultimately, is about saving the world.*

When I was a young man during my existence in Atlantis I was torn between what I wanted to do. I was fascinated by the way that things worked – why things worked as they did. I was drawn in two directions: I was drawn towards our scientific side but I was also drawn to our spiritual side. Now you must understand that in my society both sides were really one, but you could say we chose to 'major' in something: we could choose to be spiritual and major in science or we could choose to be scientific and major in the spiritual side.

I was fascinated with directions, with points on the compass, with lands 'out there', with the people we could meet... and there were frequent visitors. We denied nothing to anyone but they had to ask, because our society was more advanced than many of the societies around us. If they asked us we would show them every one of our 'secrets' – it was our spiritual duty, we felt, to share the knowledge we had with others.

I have to say that, as I grew older, religion (the religion I was brought up with, which was not religion as you would understand the term) won the upper hand with me; ritual won the upper hand with me. We had great temples and in our temples you could *see* spiritual energy because we had devices that would focus spiritual energy …focus is the wrong word… that would acoustically allow the vision of spiritual energy. This is something you don't know about today: that if you build your churches in a certain way, with a certain resonance, using certain materials, then it is easy for people who are discarnate to manifest because the acoustics, the spiritual acoustics, the vibrational acoustics, are right, they are correct. So, we had great churches where you could see balls of energy, where you could see visions if you were so inclined. I *was* so inclined and I would kneel there and I would look into the centre of the sphere of energy and I would commune with angels. I would commune with what you would call '*saints*' – evolved beings – and my life was a joyous one… until the time when everyone got it wrong.

Man's potential is equal to mine; it is equal to what I was and am capable of, to what my people were capable of. But there is at the moment also a great potential for destruction. Destruction has come to the Earth before – at least twice that I can speak about. It came during the time when I was in Atlantis but it also came long before that time. Man is far older in physical form than you realise and my reason for visiting you and expending so much energy (because communicating in this way is not a pleasant sensation for me) is *to make sure that there is not a third time.*

So, in introduction I have told you a little about myself and my background. I have always believed in my God and I am doing this (something that I have never said in earlier communications), *I am doing this at God's behest.* He wishes me to do this. How do I know?

Because I talk to Him, because my heart is so attuned to God-Vibration that I can discern His wishes and have known for a long time that these books had to be written.

Everything I will present to you in the following chapters is for you to balance, for you to measure. Nothing I say to you is a command. Everything I say to you is the truth as I see it from my vantage point. You are free to dismiss it if you wish. This is not a religious dictate – there is no penalty for disbelieving. The only penalty if you are a thinking person (and by reading this book you have proven that you are a thinking person), the only penalty is that if you do not listen to the *trumpet call* and take action personally then your world will be in increasing trouble.

I bless you for reading this book and I tell you that you have great power. This book places power in your hands – not in the hands of the church, not in the hands of the town hall. You are the point and the circle, as am I, and I wish us to work together to bring Light into your physical and spiritual existences.

Chapter 2

You are dreaming reality

Michael's notes. There is very little for me to add by way of introduction to this chapter, except to note that this was the last communication I would ever receive from *Joseph* clairaudiently, all subsequent ones being given whilst I was in a trance state.

Joseph speaks. I would like to speak to you today about dreams and about the nature of dreams and the potency of dreams. For every soul, from the most advanced through to the soul who is newly created from God and who has just incarnated onto a physical plane, *dreaming is the only means of expressing existence*. Each of us dreams throughout our lives, throughout our existences, and in dreaming creates a pattern around ourselves, which also interpenetrates the patterns of other dreamers to form what we call 'reality'.

The dreamer never really becomes involved with the dream. If you are watching a film on your level you can experience the emotions of that film, you can experience the highs and the lows, but you are not in the film, you are not really part of the film. So it is with the human spirit (with any spiritual expression from God). The pattern is created by the dreamer but *the dreamer is not the dream*. The dreamer is watching the dream in order to have experiences, in order to build into him/herself more Light.

The problem with the Earth at this present time is that the dreamers have forgotten that they are dreaming and they believe that the dream around them – the 'film' around them – is actually reality. It is not! Furthermore, the dreamers are dreaming the *wrong dream*: they are dreaming a dream of violence, and depravity, and lack, and loss, and disease.

My purpose in creating a second book is to show men and women their potential as dreamers but first of all I have to convince them that they are dreamers.

I would use the analogy of men and women going to sleep at night, because at night you experience all kinds of images that play out around you, all kinds of adventures, and yet when you wake up you do not consider yourself to have been a part of them, do you? But they are so real for you whilst you are experiencing them: you can walk down streets, you can interact with people, you can feel pain, you can feel joy, you can feel love and then you wake up and where has it gone? Where has that dream gone that engaged you to such a great extent? It was never there. It was a projection around you by your unconscious mind.

When you are awake the same thing is happening, from waking up in a morning until going to bed at night you are involving yourself in a waking dream, but it is a dream of the *conscious mind* as well as the subconscious mind, because you are projecting into the pattern – the field that is around you – what you expect from life. And, because you are conditioned by society, you expect the worst from life: you expect illness; you expect pain; you expect loss and, as a dreamer, whatever you dream will *always* come up to your expectations.

…Always!

Perfectly!

So, in the measure that you suffer you have first *wanted* that suffering (or, I should say – I should correct myself and say: 'expected that suffering'). So you expect pain and you receive it; you expect discord and you receive it; you expect from the world at large (not just from your own lives but from the world at large) there to be violence, there to be upset, there to be anger; you expect people to treat you badly; you expect nations to treat other nations badly; you expect there to be torture; you expect there to be all manner of base things happening – *and so those things happen.*

In this second book *I want to teach you how to change the dream* and it is a simple thing – you can change the dream at any time in your life, during any day. I want to give to you an exercise to prove to you that you can change the dream...

I want you to put your hand on your wrist and I want you to feel your own pulse and then I want you to tell yourself that you are healthy, that your pulse is regular, that you are feeling *great* and that there is, coming to you from God, a great deal of health on this particular day. That on this particular day everything will go right: on this particular day everybody will speak to you nicely, everybody will treat you with respect, good things will happen to you, you will be free from aches and pains; with every breath you take you will be more invigorated. And I want you set off on this day with these things in mind and *I guarantee* that, if you leave your normal dream behind – if you invest in this little fantasy of mine for twenty four hours, you will feel so much better. Good things will come to you. The telephone will ring and somebody will make you feel good. Things will happen to you at work that will be positive. There will be a spring in your step. You will forget your *imagined age*. You will feel young again; you will feel energised.

I want *each of you* to try this.

Maybe some of you reading this book are currently terribly depressed, terribly down, terribly oppressed, and maybe you feel that a day is an unimaginable length of time in which to feel good, in which to place your trust in things going well (rather than going wrong). Then try it for an hour. Try it for an hour in the morning and an hour in the afternoon and an hour before you go to bed. And for that hour say to yourself, 'I am taking time off. I am taking time off from my normal dream to dream something different, to dream something positive,' and you will find that during that hour and by the end of that hour in the morning and the afternoon and the evening you will feel better *despite yourself*.

I say 'despite yourself' because your physical being with all its might will fight against this new dream, will try to convince you that you are still ill, still depressed, still lacking. But your soul will jump for joy; your soul will be powered by your subconscious will for that hour by you reiterating: 'I am well. I have abundance. Everything is going right!' And you will find that there is a duality of nature within you – that your conscious mind is saying to you, 'I am still ill,' but something within you, some spark within you is saying, 'No, everything is right – I feel better.'

This is a book for people who want to change their world, and by the world I mean your whole planet. So, if you are reading this book it is because you want to change things. To change things you have to first change yourself, because if you take into the *greater dream* your own personal dream of lack, your own personal dream of doubt, your own personal dream of ill-health, then how can you affect the *greater dream* other than in negative ways?

First you have to change your own sphere and then you enter the greater sphere – the greater pattern, the mesh, the field of people's thinking and beliefs – and you alter it because you have first altered yourself at a subconscious level, day-by-day, by believing in a *better* dream.

And it is that simple!

You simply have to detach yourself from the concept of reality being reality... because it is *not* reality: it is always a dream, it is always a construct – no matter what you see, or feel, or hear, or smell or touch – it is a construct. It is not you! It is your belief manifest and your belief comes from yourself; it comes from your parents; it comes from the man that you pass in the street who says: 'You are looking tired today.' It comes from your employer who says, 'You are not very good at this.' It comes from your news programmes where you are told that the world is running out of energy, where you are told that people are going to war and killing each other, where you are told that this is wrong with you, that is wrong with you, that you are going to suffer in this way and that way. And you take on board, you absorb, you build into your dream, images from the *greater* dream.

What I am inviting you to do is *to build images outwards into the greater dream from your personal dream.*

So we have to get back to basics and you have to understand that, as a soul you are an expression of God, a part of God, a dream, if you like, of God – because that is what you are in essence: *you are a dream of God* – God dreams you into being. He cannot separate from Himself the part of Himself that is you but He can create the *illusion* of separation by dreaming that you are separate. You create in the same way that God creates. You are part of Him; you have never been separated from Him. So, in order to think yourself separate from Him and separate from the people around you, you dream, because in 'reality' you are *not separate* from these things.

You *dream*!

As a soul – because *God* is *perfect* and you are a permanent part of God (*never* separated from Him, in truth) – *you are perfect.* You are perfectly healthy. You cannot be born, you cannot die, you cannot suffer from ill-health, you cannot suffer from the effects of other people because these things are simply dreams.

Your start point in changing the world is to remember always that *you are perfect*, that everything else is a dream, a construct, a belief; it is not really a part of you.

You set great store in your society today by the television set: by the hundreds of channels that are available to you, by the films, the music, the sounds, the sights that you can see. But, if you do not like something you are watching, you simply switch over to another channel – and that is what I am next inviting you to do.

You don't like the world, you don't like the dream, you don't like what you are seeing? *Change the channel!*

When you awaken in a morning – before you put your feet on the ground – *see the day that you want to have for yourself and for the world*. See peace in the world. See peace in your *own* affairs: in your relationships with other people, in your relationships with your house, with your office, with your car, with your kettle, with every appliance, with the things you are sitting on, the things that you walk on – see peace and harmony from them being brought to you. Expand your view towards your country and your world. See peace in your seats of government. See peace in troubled nations. Extend your vision to the Earth and see peace in the rocks, in the flowers, in the trees, in the construction of the Earth and say to yourself *(and this is important)*: 'For today this dream is mine and no other dream shall enter it!'

And, believe me, the world will try and convince you that everything is as it always has been according to the communal dream: that there *is* war, that there *is* disease, that there *is* torture, that there *is* anger, depravity, loss, lack.

You have to be brave, you have to live the dream every day – is that not one of your advertising slogans: 'live the dream'? You have to live your new dream, God's dream for you, your dream for yourself – *that everything is fine, everything is perfect* – and you have to build it into yourself day after day after day.

At first it will be difficult because you have to change the resonance of your thoughts. It is like loading a different DVD, a different tape into a player. You have to put it in, it has to be switched on, it has to be viewed, you have to get to the right section of it – so it takes time. So, yes, expect immediate results – you must do that – but also be patient and loving with yourself and do not give up if, immediately, your day does not bring to you that ideal of the dream that you have put into it in the morning.

It will – little by little – it *will*!

You will build into yourself health; you will build into yourself an understanding of yourself and your God; you will build into yourself (and this is most important) *an understanding that what you see around you is not really there, is malleable, is able to be manipulated, able to be changed. You are the dreamer!*

And then, as you gradually change your frequency, your thoughts, your beliefs, your dreams will link up with similar dreams around the world – with the dreams of other men and women who are changing this world by being something different, by dreaming a different dream. And little by little you will then infiltrate the illusion of The Field and you will change it from within.

This is rebellion from within.

When enough people dream the dream of perfection, and peace, and holiness, and Godliness – then The Field will have no choice but to change because the majority of the thoughts that are feeding it will be infusing it with the dream of this better place.

This, Ladies and Gentlemen, is how you are going to change your world. It is a revolution but a bloodless one – and it is no use reading this book and then saying: 'I will leave it to the politicians. I will leave it to those who know better than me.' Who knows better than you? You are God!

If you want this world to change, you – and no-one else – have to change it and the change begins with the dream.

Actually (as I have said in my previous book) there is *'no-thing'* there; each morning is a blank slate. What are you then going to create today? Are you going to create a world that damages you and damages other people? Or are you going to create a world that uplifts you, that brings you closer to God in thinking, that helps you to remember who you are, that allows you to extend Light and Love to people and them to give it back to you?

I must talk for a little while about your children because they are the new dreamers; they are bringing into being *tomorrow*. Try hard not to inflict them with the lies of today. Try hard, as they grow, not to inflict them with the belief that they will grow old and die; that they will grow old and be in pain. Try hard not to inflict them with a sense of inferiority, with a sense that they can never dream and achieve anything more than you have done. That is not true.

Encourage their dreaming. Encourage the manifestation of the new spiritual awareness that is coming through the next generation of souls. Encourage them to talk to the God within. Encourage them to see the spirits who come to talk to them. Encourage them to think good thoughts. Do not make them competitive in the worldly sense – make them competitive only as soldiers for the Light, competitive in changing the status quo. And so you will be creating a new dream yourself and bringing your children into that dream so that they can reinforce and extend the new dream that changes the world.

You may say to yourself, having read this chapter: 'I am perfectly alright in my little corner.'

Are you?

Are you truly happy?

If you sit down quietly and examine your life are you happy or are you afraid? Are you happy for today but frightened that tomorrow will take away what you have today?

How long will your little corner exist? Everything changes. Everyone changes; everyone travels and moves on to different dreams. 'I am separate from people,' you may say. 'I am OK. I don't care about anyone else.' In not caring about anyone else you do not care for yourself because *you are everyone else. There is only you – the you that exists around this planet as millions of souls. Only you!* You think that you are separate from other aspects of yourself because of the illusion of The Field, because of the dream.

I am inviting you *do* something. Is it so much to ask that you see your world as perfect and holy and God-like? Isn't that what you would want for other people and for yourself? ...I take a crowbar to prise you out of your corner; to invite you to change things for everyone.

The dream at the moment is heading for cataclysm.

Cataclysm!

You can stop that! You, each of you, can stop the end of the world!

Each of you, by dreaming the right dream, prolongs the time until the end of the world – until such time as sufficient Light can come in and change that ending because it is not inevitable. *Not yet!*

But if dreamers keep dreaming the same dream then this world – as far as you are concerned, as far as the human race is concerned – *will end* …and end fairly quickly.

Do you want that? Then change things! Change things: love this planet – the planet needs Love. The dreamers have tortured this world for thousands of years. Tortured a spirit! God cannot allow that to continue; you will be called to different dreams.

So, step one is to change the way that you perceive things. There will be other steps as this book progresses but, please, I ask you each day *to see the best world that you can possibly imagine*: a world where there is no violence, where people love each other; a world where there is support for each other; a world where the only demand on people is that they be who they really are and revel in that.

It is strange, isn't it? My task is to awaken the 'sleepers' and you think that you are awake… but *you are not!* I am penetrating your dream now; the words I bring to you come from outside the perceived reality of The Field, which is only a dream. And *I* exist within a dream and *God* exists within a dream – that is how we measure ourselves, that is how we measure consciousness. We dream; we bring forth constructs from nothing. We bring forth existence from nothing – and think that these things are separate from God.

No! Your earthly existence is a dream.

It is time to change your viewpoint.

Chapter 3

You change 'The Field' through joy

Michael's notes. This was the first *Joseph* communication that involved me in the 'channelling' of a chapter. For the duration of the dictation *Joseph* delivered his words by taking control of my physical body and mind, with me being placed in a trance state so that he could 'step in' and talk to us. This delicate connection was severed momentarily on three occasions, possibly because this was the first time that *Joseph* and I had worked together in this way, and *Joseph's* linking comments at the points at which this happened are indicated in the text. He also mentions atmospheric conditions impeding the usual smooth flow of communication.

Included at the end of this chapter are questions from David and Jane and *Joseph's* response to these. From this point onwards *Joseph* repeatedly invited and openly encouraged questions to be asked following the delivery of each chapter. His answers always proved to be highly informative and provided further insights into the topic he had chosen to talk about on each occasion. Subsequent question and answer sessions are therefore included where appropriate throughout the rest of this book at the end of the relevant chapters.

Joseph speaks. In this session I would like to speak about *joy* and about the ability of the human spirit to bring forth joy. You might think that that is a trivial subject to talk about in a book that is intended to change the Earth but it is one of the most important factors in Creation and one of the factors that is missing most from people's souls and from their approach to the Earth and to their lives at this time – and it has been missing since the time of The Fall.

*God is joy*ous – again one of my statements – *God is joy*ous. I said in the previous book that God is a circle, but God is also joy. *God, principally, is joy.* You can say, 'Well, God is happiness, God is sadness, God is all the other emotions that apply to the human being,' but I would say, 'No. Principally *God is joy because Creation is joy.*'

In the beginning – in the beginning of time as you measure it on this level of consciousness – God brought forth *joy. Light is joy.* Light – when applied to any situation, to any human being, any soul, any conflict – is joy. God's natural state is one of bliss, one of joy, one of happiness – *extreme happiness.* In the beginning God imbued His children (because they *were and are* His children – a part of Him) with a joy at being in the physical universe, a joy at approaching their lives and discovering the things that were intended to be discovered on a physical plane.

Discontent then grew through the minds of men as the balance of The Field (the field of *joy*, of course, that was created by human beings in the beginning) was gradually changed through the discontent that came to a few with obstinate minds and a strong intention to know better than God and to do better than God. And so *the balance was tipped* and, as people began to experience the darker side of Creation, the darker possibilities, then those vibrations were also poured into The Field so The Field itself became polluted. The field of creative joy became a field of pain and of suffering.

In this particular chapter I want to underline the fact that *suffering does not come from God. God knows nothing about suffering or pain; that is not God's natural state and it is not the natural state of His children.*

Many of your religions are built around the concept that God wants people on Earth to suffer. This, children; this, priests; this, ministers; this, religious fanatics, is a nonsense! *God does not want any of His children to suffer*. God's vibration is so far above that of suffering that He cannot even conceive of what suffering is. He only feels, perceives, the need of His children for Him. I want you to understand that God does not feel apart from His children, He does not feel separated from them. It is the reverse that is true: *His children, deep within their souls, feel separated from Him and He perceives that within His creative field*, within His creative aura, if you like.

So suffering is created (I want to underline this as well), *suffering is created by man; has always been created by man*. Man tipped the balance by being impatient; by thinking that he knew more than God and, by doing so, poured his impatience into The Field. That impatience was then perceived by other human beings around the world who also became impatient and who then became upset. They poured more negativity into The Field that God have given them to enable them to create whatever they wanted to create, and The Field turned from one of positivity to one of negativity.

Your Field now is one of suffering: it is one of depression and depravity and poverty and violence, but God has not created this state. What a popular phrase is: 'Why does God let this happen?' *He lets this happen because you are His children* – He cannot go against Himself, He cannot intercede against Himself and you are part of Him. He waits patiently and instructs through His angels and through His ministers of Light so that there will come a time *when you will turn that field around again; when you will stop the suffering; when you will stop it happening.*

Why, Brothers and Sisters, do *you* let it happen? – That is a better question!

Because, for one, you do not know better …but you know better now, don't you, because I'm telling you this! *You create the suffering around the world* – every murder, every time someone is tortured, every time someone is robbed, every time someone is sexually abused. Maybe to only an infinitesimally small degree but you contribute to these things because you contribute to The Field with your thoughts. And you will say, 'I am not a murderer! I am not a torturer! I have never abused anybody.' No, as an individualisation of God you haven't, but your thoughts contribute to The Field that some draw on more heavily than others.

If you take away that charge of negativity from The Field then you would be surprised at how quickly those crimes of violence and violent acts would disappear because they would have no power – which brings me back to joy and the need for joy in everything that you do. If you daily practise a code of joy then you put into The Field positivity and Light and more of what God is about, and you push away from The Field the darkness, the suffering, the need to buy into negativity and upset every day of your lives.

How can you be joyous when The Field tells you that you are miserable? Well, when you wake up in the morning you say to yourself: 'I am alive – thank you, Father! And I am happy that I am alive; and I am happy that I am me; and I am happy that God has given me this opportunity to grow on this physical plane during this day.' Then you should notice – *really notice* – the things around you during that day that bring you joy. You have a beautiful sphere, a beautiful planet. It has within it plant life, animal life, bird life, marine life that is a joy to behold – different expressions of God you could study for eons and still find fascinating.

But instead you put your blinkers on as you go to work and see nothing of the joy that is around you. Look up! Look up at the clouds and the sky and see the beauty inherent in such aspects of Creation. Be joyous! Be joyous that your heart beats from minute to minute without you having to think about it; that your thoughts flow from one thought to another without you consciously having to go through that process; that you can breathe; that you can touch and feel and smell and taste; and that you are an infinite being.

Also view on this special, joyous day every person that you come across as part of your family… because they are! And say, 'There is such joy that I am part of that person on the other side of the street who is hurrying to work. There is such joy in…

…I am sorry, Michael touched something, which momentarily withdrew the link…

…the person I am talking to across the Post Office counter, in the person who is in front of me in the car, in the people who are in the bus behind me. There is such joy that these are different aspects of God – all with potential; such joy in being part, ultimately, of a plan to raise the consciousness of this Earth and the people who live on it.'

Then, you should also have joy in saying: 'I am fulfilling God's plan. I do not know what that plan is but there is joy because in my heart God will plant a seed and tell me what to do daily.' You should have joy in that too.

You would think that this was the *easiest* way out of your present predicament on Earth (and it is from a spiritual point of view) but from your point of view, from the human point of view, it is one of the hardest things to do.

I want you to spend a second day (having spent a day in joy); I would like you to spend a day in *observation* and, from rising from your beds in the morning to going back to them at night, I want you to see how many miserable people there are on Earth. Listen when somebody phones you and see what lies behind their words. Watch your television, watch your dramas, and see what your dramas are centred upon. See in the workplace how people are reacting to their day. See how many people ignore you as you smile at them in the street. I want you to be aware of the effects of The Field and there is no better way to become aware of them than to tune in and really observe for a whole day. *By doing this you will really observe the need for change and really observe how many people are thoroughly upset, depressed, miserable, hopeless.*

People should be carefree – free of cares. Isn't it said in the Bible that God takes care of you; that every hair on your head is numbered; that not a sparrow falls without God knowing about it; that the lilies of the field are taken care of? But you do not listen. Mankind does not listen. Mankind is *content* in its misery, content to steer its own miserable path.

What I am suggesting is that first you see how true that is because the chances are that you are also locked into this world and have never thought about it in this way. I want you to observe, to see, how upset most people are ...and then *I want you to do something about it.* And the 'something' you can do is to *live your life in joy, because in living your life in joy you change your world by putting positivity into The Field.* You then prepare yourself for greater gifts because, as God observes (through being part of you) that you are raising your vibrations through being joyous, He can then send you messengers from the spirit spheres – messengers who will instruct you, who will inspire you, so that you can *see* the angel by your side, you can *see* the path ahead of you and you can *feel* from within yourself what to do in all circumstances.

Strangely, you might think that elevating yourself raises your vibration and quickens your vibration – it does – but there is a paradox in that, *as your vibration quickens, you slow down.* Part of what is wrong with your world today is that everything goes at such a speed.

And that is strange because if people stopped; if people were quiet for a few moments, for an hour, for a day; if they really took a week off and said: 'This is a holiday from the world, I am going to be quiet, I am going to indulge in joy,' then…

…Sorry, I had disconnected with Michael again…

…if people were to take time off their vibrations would rise… but they would do so *as a result of the person slowing down. So the molecules of their body would speed up but the effect on their lives would be to slow them down.*

There is misery for a reason; people indulge in misery, misery and *more misery.* Speed is all around you for a reason – speed, speed, *speed* – the reason being that speed does not allow you to stop. If you stop then God can get in, so your society is geared towards misery; it says: 'Come on, be fast, keep going, there is so much to do,' because it *knows* (remember, The Field is *conscious*) that if you slow down you will let God in. And that is an echo back to The Fall. The souls involved in The Fall did not want to let God in – they wanted to push God out, wanted to become Gods themselves (ironically not realising that they already were).

So I want you to look at that seeming paradox: *in order to evolve your molecules have to rise to a higher vibrationary rate, yes, but in order to evolve you – as spirits – need to slow down.* If you slow down you, in effect, step outside of The Field so that you can look at The Field from an observer's point of view rather than being a part of it. You are always a contributor to it, but in slowing down, in meditating, in stepping back from it, you contribute peace to it – a slower vibration.

There is a need for joy; there is a need for progress through slowing down. Where do you feel your world is going? At its present speed where is it rushing to? Considering that you go nowhere anyway, where are you all rushing to? What is it you wish to achieve... heart disease, brain tumours, cancer? What is this speed giving you? And, considering that you will go back to a spiritual sphere at the end of your small life on Earth, what do you hope to achieve? Do you wish to be managing director of the world, the top of your tree? This again is an echo back to The Fall where everyone wanted to be important – more important than God.

There is nothing more important than God because *God is what you are*. Therefore you have to slow down and, in slowing down, you will still achieve the things in life that you wish to achieve but you will put into The Field the right kind of vibration – joy, upliftment – and banish the suffering from The Field.

With many souls, because of the speed of their lives, they are propelled (almost literally) into the next life without stopping to think. The slowing down I am talking about also applies to the life immediately after this one – that time when you will contemplate what you have done and what you are going to do. Many people go so fast, want so much, that they take with them when they die, when they pass into the next stage of contemplation, that speed – that desire to keep going, to keep going *fast* – and that very often brings them back to the Earth plane for *more of the same*.

Sadly, this also applies to violence. The violent man and woman can become so enmeshed in a violent way of life that they are propelled – reincarnated – into another violent way of life. True, the Lords of Karma try to imbue that next life with some pointers, some points of change that will allow the spirit to escape the cycle it has put itself into. But contemplate what a terrible thing this is: that the speed that seems to be so important on your planet and the violence that you want to rid yourselves of often propel souls into a further incarnation, during which they will encounter much the same kind of existence.

It is time to be quiet, to be still, to meditate, to contemplate, to let God in!

I, in certain distant parts of my infinite existence, was a violent man (I am going back many, many years), but following The Fall there was a different vibration to the Earth and I see the violence that I quickly got out of my system now being *instilled* into people. Many of the young people you see now that are so violent were violent in their last life – that is why they are so violent in this life – and you can see that The Field is preparing them for more violence. *The Field is becoming an increasingly violent field as well as a rapid and a depressed one.* So The Field is nurturing their violence and there seems to be no-one making a stand against this. Your policing methods are inadequate, your politics are haphazard because there is no-one with the heart to put joy into things at the level at which people try and take control of the violence…

…I am sorry – my connection with Michael keeps disconnecting… almost disconnecting…

…The atmospheric conditions are not perfect today but I hope I have got across what I am trying to say to you. In the first book it must have seemed as though I was criticising so many areas of your world but I have to de-construct before I can construct: I have to tell you what is wrong before I can tell you how to put it right. This second book is about putting it right – *a practical guide to changing your world*. It is about practical things that ordinary men and women can do to change your world so that we can get in; so that God, if you like, can reclaim His children by re-connecting with them in a stronger way than He does now. I had better explain that: most souls are not aware that they are part of God. God is always connected to them; God has never lost them. They have lost themselves; they have placed themselves in an area of deprivation through thought, through volition, through perception. It is not that God needs to reconnect with His children – His children need to reconnect *consciously* with Him.

…Are there any questions on the subject I have spoken about today?

David. It seems to me that people get into what I call a 'feedback loop' and they keep feeding the violence and the depression and really what you are saying is that they need to break that feedback loop and set up a new one in the other direction. So, instead of it enforcing negativity, it needs to enforce positivity – and this is the difficulty in breaking the feedback loop from our point of view.

Joseph. That is exactly it. There is an analogy I would like to give. Most children at one stage or another reach out their hand and touch fire and then very quickly learn that that is not the thing to do, and that knowledge remains with them for the rest of their incarnation. The analogy is that in The Fall the souls involved, in effect, touched fire – created fire around themselves – but kept touching fire to the point where it numbed them… so they *expected* to touch fire, they *expected* pain because that is what they had created. And you are quite right – it is a circle, it is a cyclic pattern of degradation, of upset.

Built into the human consciousness is an *expectation of life being miserable* now: of life bringing people illness and violence; that they should fear for their existence and for their next meal and for a bed to sleep in and a house to live in. This has taken place for so long that it is indeed a cycle and souls are reborn into it because their expectation is so strong that, when they come to the spirit side of life, the teams of people here who work with them to try and change their perceptions *cannot get in*. The best they can do – and here there is another analogy I can make – is to pack a suitcase for those souls that is loaded with 'good things' so that they can take that suitcase into their next incarnation and open it at pre-determined points in order to learn the lessons that will move them away from the cycle they have got themselves into.

So, yes, we have to break, or, rather, *you* have to break – I cannot do it for you – you human beings have to break the cycle. But in order to do that you first have to recognise that a cycle is there and that is one of our most difficult tasks – teaching you to perceive things as being wrong. Most people shrug their shoulders and get on with life and say, 'Well, I have had a good innings. I am now ill, I am now dying, I haven't any money, things are wrong with me,' and accept it. Our task is to say, 'Don't accept it – it is a lie. Don't accept it – you can regenerate, you can heal yourself; you can heal this world!'

You are not at the mercy of The Field, you are not at the mercy of society – you are at the mercy of yourself; *you* decide what happens to you, although mostly subconsciously. What is happening to you today has been decided by your past actions, perhaps in another lifetime. You are experiencing what you are experiencing presently because your past actions have placed you in your present circumstances so that you can learn from them... what is happening to you now – how you approach it and how you transmute it – is for *the good of your soul*. And that is ironic, isn't it, because you would say that in most lives people are simply enduring their experiences, and learning from them for the good of their soul is the last thing on their minds. As guides we try to make people see the truth of their situation, try to make them react in different ways, to evolve spiritually, but we can often only influence them from within – via their intuition – by a tiny degree during each life and over the course of many lives – I have to correct myself because, of course, there are many souls who *do* illuminate, self-illuminate, during their lives and then pass onto higher spheres of consciousness or, bravely, as you have done (*Michael: Joseph is referring to the sitters*), choose to come back to teach the others what they have learned.

There is an analogy with you saying 'cycles', David, where you could say that you are driving a car and that the wheels are going forwards all the time and what I am trying to teach you is *to put the brakes on*, because if you put the brakes on you might be able to pull off the motorway into a beautiful little spot, a beautiful lay-by, and see things in a different way.

First you have to put the brakes on. The speed of your world is burning up the physical body; is burning up the planet; you are running out of resources. You are running out of mental resources because all you think of doing is to build another chemical plant or make another material that defoliates the world or uses up the oil supplies.

You are running out of ideas. We seek to provide you with new ideas to ensure that the balance is changed on this Earth. We don't often say this but, *looking at your world from a spiritual point of view, we see almost a blackened cinder – the vibrations of the Earth are so dense.* I know that from space your world looks like a jewel but that is its spirit shining out. If you were to look at it on a level of spiritual perception of the human field it would seem to you to be twisted and painful and misty and dark.

And that is why communication with the spirit worlds is so difficult, because in order to talk to you we have to *bring Light – energy – with us* – there is not enough Light on your level to sustain communication. The difficulty lies not in you struggling to perceive us as nebulous 'ghosts or spirits', it lies in a dependency on our Light to allow communication to take place, because yours alone cannot sustain it. We therefore have to generate a great deal of power. That is why we always say at services (*Michael: a reference to spiritualist services*) that people should join together to produce Light... but they don't; they only take. Spirit communication should be (and is intended to be) a staple part of everyday life on Earth. It was once – it was in my time – and *it has to be again.*

Is there anything else you would like to discuss?

Jane. You said that God doesn't know anything of suffering but does He suffer when we suffer? Is He aware of every individual's suffering?

Joseph. He is aware of the predicament of each of His children but by His nature He is joy, He is upliftment, He is creativity and Light. So His problem, if you like – if God can have a problem, lies in trying to give the best to His children but not being able to present it to His children in the form that it exists in because the Light that God *is* will not 'fit' into the human soul. The human soul is below that Light and has to come upwards to that Light. God cannot diminish what He is – *He simply is.* He does not seek to diminish Himself or change Himself in that way.

The children of God need to expand, to open themselves up to His goodness, and so God 'drip-feeds' opportunities to learn to His children. He places opportunities in front of them that strangely, very often through suffering, break away that suffering and lift the soul upwards. He has to communicate with them on their level as well as His but He cannot give them the Light that is on His level as it is. It would blind them. It would *destroy* them. They are vessels that cannot contain that Light as it is, so the Light has to be slowed down; the Light has to be 'darkened', and it is through experience that God brings back His children to His home.

Does God weep for His children? God's children – a part of Him weep – so He is weeping. God's children suffer – so He is suffering. But there are multiple levels to God's consciousness and God is aware on many levels: God can see His child as what it *was* – a part of Him; as what it *is* – a part of Him; and as what it will be – a glorious part of Him *all at the same time*. So the suffering that you are talking about with regard to each soul is only a period within that soul's infinite existence. And, yes, He sees it, but He is always working *joyously* to elevate each soul through the experiences that are brought to it through the Lords of Karma who incarnate that soul into the best circumstances in order that those experiences can manifest themselves around and through that soul.

The Field is almost anti-God, if you like. The Field is a creation of the human condition. It is almost an exclusion of God and that, of course, is a result of what the souls in The Fall did – they excluded themselves from God. They created that field and, because it was a conscious wish – 'We know better than God, we will create a society that is better than God's society, a state of mind that is better than God's state of mind' – they built into The Field that wish to be excluded from God, that wish to move away from God because 'they knew better'... and that resonance is still within The Field.

So you have a state of being that *God cannot really penetrate* because, whilst it is of His children, *it is not of Him*; it is not of His ideals or His intent. This is why Light has to be 'drip-fed', has to be pin-pointed here and there to change that field and to consciously bring back the children of God into God's community. You must remember that God's community does not just comprise of human beings; there are other physical manifestations of the soul living on other planets, other spiritual manifestations of the soul living in other areas of the spirit worlds.

So, God is trying to bring His children on Earth (and in the surrounding area of space) back into the fold. But He can only do that, because of His nature, by presenting His children with Himself, not by changing that which is not Him, which is only an illusion, a shadow. He will not change it because it is not of Him, it does not really exist – which comes back to what we were saying in the first book – that *nothing really exists except the Light, except God*. So God has no need to change – it is His children who need to change. Is there anything else?

Jane. No.

(Michael: at this point the meeting was closed with a prayer.)

Chapter 4

Tear down your walls!

Michael's notes. Half way through this fourth chapter *Joseph* mentions a word that can sometimes strike fear into the hearts of spiritual seekers… *meditation*. Mistakenly, many people consider this to be a frustrating subject that is hopelessly complex and beyond their capabilities. Can I therefore reassure you with a few words regarding meditation at this point so that you can approach the exercise in this chapter, and the other examples in this book, without worry and in a way that will bring you great satisfaction and reward?

Meditation is neither difficult nor complex, nor is it something that need take up oodles of your personal time. When undertaken using visualisation (transcendental or mystical meditation is a subject for a whole other book!) meditation could be described as 'imagining with a positive attitude' – it's as simple as that. As long as you approach each of your meditations by asking God to protect you and to guide you, and ask for the same thing when you end the exercise, also asking Him to close your chakras for you, you will find the exercises calming and beneficial. Chakras, by the way, are your body's principal spiritual energy centres or vortices, which will usually 'open' during your meditations, as the act of mentally sidestepping this world and contemplating spiritual matters activates them, so that you can receive energy and inspiration. You don't need to worry about, study or understand everything about them, it's enough that you ask and trust

Higher Authority to close them for you when coming out of a meditation, and to then spend a couple of peaceful minutes allowing this to be done for you before you take up your daily tasks again.

Joseph gives you powerful images to follow throughout each of his meditations. The one he offers here is a liberating and healing tool, formulated to contribute positively to your life, and an essential aspect of the topic he is covering – that of the restrictive 'walls' we create around ourselves and the steps we can take to tear them down.

What may lose a little in the translation from spoken to written word here is *Joseph*'s absolute *passion* for his God and his subject and his absolute belief that mankind needs to change. He pulls no punches in delivering what he has to say; he 'tells it like it is' and is adamant that people should review the way they approach life *now* as time is of the essence...

At the end of the session our group was given further advice by *Joseph* regarding how to get his first book – **Revelation: Joseph's Message** – out into the world. We include much of that information here as it resonates with the theme of this chapter and offers the reader valuable information that can be applied to any project in life.

Joseph speaks. The title of this chapter is 'walls'. I want to speak today about the walls – the barriers – that you put up between each other.

Of course, in the beginning, barriers were necessary to create, as it were, a dividing line between what was you and what was not you. And the initial phase of that was to decide that you were separate from God so that you could experience things from your own point of view. But, as time has progressed on your world, more and more divisions and walls have been and continue to be put up between each of you.

First of all, you have an *emotional* barrier – you do not let other people in. Your emotions, you feel, are *private*, as though no one else has ever experienced them and they are therefore a precious thing that no one else should have *access* to. So, instead of stating what you truly feel, you erect a barrier, a wall, and you say, 'Thus far and no further towards my emotions. You are not going to be let in. I may place 'doors' in the wall to give you glimpses of who I really am, but for the most part you are shut out.'

You then erect a wall *mentally* and you say: 'You cannot scale the heights of my intellect. You must stay outside of my intellect because your intellect is not equal to mine and your understanding is not equal to mine,' and very often there are no doors in this wall at all.

Then you erect another wall in terms of *status* and you say: 'This is mine. This is an expression of me and it is a wall that keeps you out because you are not able to attain what I have attained materially. You cannot have the same car I have. You cannot have the same lifestyle or house that I have. I have erected another barrier that you cannot get through.'

And then there is a *racial* wall you build, and you say: 'I am not the same as you – you frighten me. I am not the same as you – I am *better* than you! My way – my racial tendencies – are better than yours. You therefore do not get in! You do not mix with me – I have built a wall.'

And then there is a *religious* wall where you say, 'This is my religion, this is the *one* religion. This religion keeps you out because you are not of this religion,' and you erect a further wall in this way.

Then there is a *spiritual* wall – there is a wall that says: 'I am alive now and I will not think about death until I am on my deathbed and I cannot countenance anything to do with spirituality. And so I have built a wall and, on that side is whatever comes next and on this side here I am and I am safe.'

And then you build an *inner* wall and you say: 'The things that have happened to me in life are *too painful*. As a result there is a wall I built when I was fifteen and something I found hard to cope with happened; there is a wall I built when I was twenty-three and another difficult something happened; there is a wall I built when I was thirty for similar reasons, and I will not revisit those times. These are barriers, built to restrain those things I do not wish to hurt me. I have built them to keep terrible experiences *out* – even though the walls are *inside* of me.'

So, from the time you are born you begin to build walls. Since you began to populate this planet and began to build you have actually built *physical* walls across continents, across countries, across towns and cities, to keep out the *intruder*, to keep in the 'sacredness' of what you are.

You build walls around your hearts and your minds and your families and your houses and your cities and your countries and your races.

If your world is to change then walls have to come down!

If your world is to change you have to appreciate each other's cultures and tolerate each other's cultures. If your world is to change you have to realise that intellect is only a façade; that the person you meet who may not appear to be 'up to your intellect' may be the highest spiritual being you have ever come across. If your world is to change you have to expose your hearts and your minds and say: 'This is what I really want: I want peace – not war. I want love.'

That is the *biggest* wall of all – the pretence that you do not want or need love. You are part of God and God is Love. In building that first wall that separated you from God in consciousness (although it does not really exist), you separated yourself from *Love*. If you cannot admit to yourselves that you need Love then your world will never change for the better; it will *continue* to change for the worse.

Here is a thought for you to contemplate, to meditate on: *every act on your level that appears to be born out of evil is – initially – born as a seed thought out of a need for love*, a need for security; a need to feel safe. In not admitting that you need love you push away everything that is different and you perpetuate the state of affairs you find on this planet at the moment.

You need God's Love.

You need each other's Love.

A child needs Love, needs guidance, and you give your Love to children so easily as parents. But then you wean the child off Love. You say: 'You must now take your place in the world and it is a bad place, it is a difficult place. You cannot wear your heart on your sleeve; you cannot go around loving people. You will get hurt.'

I tell you: *you will never get hurt in loving people.* You may have challenging circumstances arise because you have tried to do your best, because you have tried to love other people, but you will never get hurt. Your soul will never get hurt. In fact, *the greatest protection you can ever give to your soul is Love:* loving the person who hates you (the Master said this), turning the other cheek, living in Love, realising that you need Love, that you need God.

In order to change, each person reading this book has to make the admission: 'I need Love.'

Is it not said that *no man is an island*? You need each other. You need that Love vibration in your heart, in your soul. Then you will realise why you act in certain ways; why you seek as nations to suppress and oppress other nations; why you try to gather around yourself so much in the way of materialism that fails to make you happy; why you build barriers to keep out that which you perceive as not being able to bring you security or Love. You mature the day that you understand that you need Love – then you start to take the walls down. Your society needs not walls but God – the God it has distanced itself from.

The second thing you have to contemplate, need to meditate on (and it has been said so many times but not understood) is that, if you want Love, in order to find it you *first have to give it away*.

…*You have to give it away*.

You cannot give it away if you have built walls around yourself.

If you do not like a situation simply *love it away* – from an illness to an irritation with someone to a group you perceive as behaving unspiritually or a sect that you do not like: love their negative effects on you away. *That which you fear, you perpetuate*. That which you have built a wall against you perpetuate because your thoughts are constantly maintaining the wall using the bricks and cement of your fear. That which you love dissipates. Because it cannot harm you it holds no fear for you, it holds no insecurity for you.

Love changes things because Love does not acknowledge, cannot be affected by, cannot give power to anything less than itself. Therefore in Love there is no war, there is no violence, there is no disease. Love is a perfect state. God-Love is a perfect state of bliss and *within that state of bliss nothing can go wrong*.

So – hold in your minds, in your meditations, those situations you wish to change *in a bubble of Love*. And you will say: 'Well, *I* cannot change things. I am just one person.' No! You are not listening to me! *You are part of God* and in being part of God *you are everything*. You are eternal Love. When you love *selflessly* (not wanting anything back) you draw on the *infinite power* of God-Love to change things, because the power of your Love is not filtered, not lessened by your perceptions of what the ego-you wants. Your desire is simply to change things into and via God-Love. So, in wielding God-Love and sending it into a situation you are 'legion', you are powerful, and you are able to *love things better.*

The more of you that do this the more quickly things will change in your world. You have to take your walls down and be brave enough to say: 'I will let people in. I will let ideas in. I will not fight against ideas.' The path of no resistance is the path of Love. Nothing can harm you if you take the walls down and, having taken them down, taken the barriers down, you will realise that your intellect does not set you apart, that your materialism does not set you apart, that your race does not set you apart, that your religious preferences do not set you apart. In realising all these things you then have *true power.*

You cannot be set apart. The walls you build are illusions. You cannot be set apart from God nor from everyone else because you are a part of them. And no matter – *listen to me* those of you who cause violence – *no matter how much you hate someone you are never apart from them.* Do you hear me? No matter how much you loathe someone, hate someone, put up barriers, wish to kill someone, *you are not apart from them.* Your own illusions cannot destroy *That Which Is* – and That Truth Which Is is that you are a part of each person you meet... and *ever more will be so.*

We have to touch here on a topic I mentioned in my first communications (*Michael*: in **Revelation: Joseph's Message**) with you – that of The Fall; that of mankind having lost its way many, many years ago. It is because of this you see yourselves as separate. Because of this act, this rashness, this problem that was created, you *strengthened* the barriers between yourselves and God – barriers that don't really exist, but from your point of view they *do* – because of what you did to the vibrations of this planet. You are investing time in perpetuating the faults that were made thousands, millions of years ago. You have to change things; you have to restore the vibrations of this planet – restore it to the paradise it was meant to be and *really is* under the layers of walls that you have built up.

You have to understand that the things you think separate you from God and from each other aren't there. That, as you read this book *you are one with everything* – not just with every other human being but with the planet, with animal life, with the universe, with the whole of Creation. It cannot be otherwise, so why invest so much of your time on Earth in building walls?

This will upset you:

Your religions are illusion; your political biases are illusion; your triumphant, flag-waving causes are illusion; your perceived hurts and hatreds are illusion... because you are living in an illusion, and, unrecognised and underlying this illusion is the Love that you are.

You are Love, capable of wielding the whole of God's Love as a tool to change this world.

A Meditation.

> What I would like you to do, as an exercise, is to sit in meditation and imagine that you are in a walled courtyard, and that outside of that courtyard is your *enemy* – perhaps it is your neighbour, or a group of people, or a concept that certain people hold dear but you don't, or someone who you perceive as having done you wrong.
>
> You will find this difficult, but on the first day of doing this meditation I want you to know that that person or that concept is standing outside of your wall ...and *to send Love to them*. Maybe you will only achieve it for a millisecond but I want you to send Love to them, please. The second

time you try this meditation it should be easier – you should be able to send more Love to them, to sustain your outpouring of Love for more than a millisecond.

I want you to continue with this meditation *until* you feel sufficiently at home with sending Love to the person (or the concept, or the group, or whatever it is that you hate), to a point where you can imagine – place – a door in your walled courtyard and know that that person is standing just behind the door.

Then – and maybe this will take you weeks, maybe months, but at some time in the future as you practise this meditation I want you to *open* that door and see the person standing there in the doorway. Maybe they will scowl at you; maybe they will have a weapon with them, but send your Love to them on that day during that meditation, knowing that they cannot harm you.

And over the months as you continue to open the door and see them standing there see them begin to change, begin to soften. Look for the God within them. Truly love them and, at a point when you can and feel you are able to, let them into – invite them into – your courtyard. Perhaps in your imagination you will sit on a bench in your courtyard. If you do so let them sit on the bench with you. Invite them to sit on the bench with you. Look for the good points in them; give them your Love, your attention, your forgiveness. *Change them and change yourself.*

You could do this with a group of people: you can see those people outside your walled courtyard and, when you have loved them sufficiently, you can let them in. You can do this meditation with anything you are frightened of, anything that upsets you. Surround the concept with Love until you are sufficiently happy with it to let it in and, in letting it in, you will see that it has no power over you and that you, in fact, have the power because you are *wielding Love*.

When you have done this with enough situations you can take down, mentally take down the walls of your walled courtyard so that you are open, so that you are loving, so that you *fear nothing and change everything*.

I am trying to get across to you the concept of transmutation, and transmutation begins within – with your concept of who you are and how you react to the situations around you. There are no situations around you – there is only You, there is only God. The *things* that are outside that walled courtyard – the things that you hate – are you!

Listen to me, terrorists! Listen to me, politicians! Listen to me, dictators! Listen to me, men and women of violence – *you are attacking yourself*. YOURSELF! And the horror that you do to 'yourself' will have to be repaid one day, will have to be transmuted. Better that it is transmuted *here* whilst you are on this planet than on the spirit side of life!

Young children have no barriers. They will happily play with children of another race, another creed. They do not look for the bad in people; they recognise the good, the Love in people. They have no sense of danger, they have no sense of threat because they have not yet been polluted by The Field, by the illusion of the planet that you have placed yourself into. This is what 'if you want to enter the Kingdom of Heaven you must be like a little child' means – you must be loving. Love takes away the barriers; there are no barriers in the first place if you love. You need to become childlike again in your approach to this world.

Know that you are operating out of fear: your violence is born out of fear – out of what you perceive to be a lack of Love; your anger is a lack of Love; your perceived hurts are a lack of Love; the illnesses you find you are suffering from are because of a perception of a lack of Love. *When you restore Love to the balance all is well, all is perfect.*

So, as you progress through life, please try the exercise of loving – in your family life, in your community life, in your connection with the rest of the world, in your metal life and in your spiritual life. And from this point onwards (as you read this) try not to build any more barriers. The thing you are trying to keep out is *yourself*; the thing you are trying to change is *yourself*; the thing you hate is *yourself*. No wonder you are ill, no wonder there is such violence – you are fighting yourself. Collectively you are in turmoil because you *know*, on a subconscious level, that you are fighting yourself.

Tear down the barriers. Tear down the walls. Take a step towards the next point in the evolution of the human race – an integrated human race that is closer to God. Lift this planet back from the brink by loving the planet too!

Joseph's information for the Band of Light:
I have been watching with interest the progress of the first communication (*Michael*: a reference to **Revelation: Joseph's Message**). I would stress that, although you feel you have in your hands physical copies of the book you don't really – you have a means of delivering the *concept*. You have the ultimate means of delivering the concept. You are about to market, to promote the book. The way to do this is through Love; is to see it in your meditations as an object of Love that you are sending out to people; to see it as bridging the gap, building bridges and tearing down the walls. With every book you send out you should also send out Love.

You should see the pile of books you have as being imbued with God's Love – because they are – and you should see the message as *already being out there* and that it is simply a matter of people *remembering* when they turn to you for a book. You should love the people you wish to take up your cause. Love the ways in which the book can get out.

The book has to be seen as something people need and that you are on a sacred mission supplying that need, fulfilling that need. And it is true – people around the world already need the book, it is simply that they do not *know* that they need the book. So you have to set up a spiritual beacon and say: 'The book is available here. Your need is fulfilled here.' Ignore the words, ignore the way the book looks – only seek to get out the concept, the Love to people and you will do us a great service by doing this.

(*Michael*: there is a very long pause from *Joseph* at this point.)

I seek sometimes to put across concepts that are beyond words into words, which is why I paused. Always we are drawing the unseen into the seen when we communicate with you and it is a difficult thing to do. Not that we are 'above you' in any way; it is just that your thoughts are locked into this illusion and our words have to convey a notion of spirituality and they fall short on this level. Were you communicating with us on our level there would be much more meaning and much more understanding to our words.

This is what I am trying to get across – that your book is 'a parcel' that takes to people the written word but also gives them the processes and the ideas and the ideals and the spirituality and the Love behind the word. You have to look beyond the words. This is what you are delivering.

If I can make you understand, the book brings to people so much more than words. It opens them up to their greater selves, to concepts and actions and a way of life they have not considered before. It is – as you have said – *a book that will change their world*. So you have to view that book as something extremely special and sacred. Then the right words will come out in your sales of it, in your promotion of it.

You have, in a way, to be blind to the illusion and say: 'This is what you need' – because it *is* what they need; *it is what they need!* They do not need ghosts and goblins (*Michael*: here *Joseph* is making reference to the many 'ghost-hunting' shows on television currently); they do not need spirit communication from the ancestors. They need to *change* – change for the better, taking away the fear, the walls I have spoken about.

Do you see that? Do you understand that?

(*Michael*: we assured *Joseph* that we did indeed understand what he was saying, and at this point the communication was broken until the next time we sat.)

Chapter 5

Be careful what you ask for

Michael's notes. This chapter had a long and unusual evolution. Firstly, on the day that he delivered it through me in trance *Joseph* initially seemed a little harder to contact and to connect with than usual. When the link was eventually established he explained that he had, just prior to visiting us, been involved in a demanding mission to try and prevent something disturbing happening on Earth.

That he had not fully delivered the concepts he wished to on this occasion did not become apparent until we were editing this chapter, at which time certain concepts did not seem, to me, to have the usual *Joseph* 'depth' to them. Contacting *Joseph* to ask for his advice, I was clairaudiently given a great number of additions to the latter half of the chapter, ultimately arriving at a piece that *Joseph* was highly satisfied with. I suppose you could therefore say that this communication is a hybrid in terms of how it arrived here – initially through trance and then being enhanced and expanded by *Joseph* through a clairaudient link at a later date.

Joseph speaks. We have had some difficulties setting up the arrangement this morning, which is nothing to do with Michael – it is actually to do with me and other things I had to do before speaking to you. I wish to ask for God's blessing on this assembly this morning as we begin and I wish to bring you all under God's protection.

I know I have touched upon the subject in the first book (*Michael*: in the chapter *Needs*) but I want to approach it from a different point of view. The thing I want to talk about today is 'lack' and its origins. I want to talk about it this time from the point of view of people's *misunderstanding* of how lack is created.

The fact is that many people, from the time they become independent of their parents until the time they 'die' to the Earth plane, are concerned, often preoccupied, with lack on a daily basis. From the moment they awaken in the morning to the moment they go back to sleep at night there is an underlying sense of loss with them; a sense of lack. For example, they feel that they do not have enough money, that there can never be enough money for them! Have you noticed how even the millionaires want *more* money? They have more money than they can *deal with* in a lifetime but they want more money! The average person – the average man or woman – is keyed into feeling that they are not rich enough.

There is also a feeling of lack with the human race in terms of health. People never feel healthy enough; they anticipate that something is bound to go wrong with them – that something is always about to go wrong with them. You would be surprised at how many people go to your doctors and say: 'I have a feeling that there is something wrong,' or, 'I haven't got enough energy,' or, 'I can't run fast enough,' or, 'I can't walk fast enough.' These are exaggerations, of course, but what I am trying to get across is that people go to the doctor because they feel there should be an underlying ideal level of energy that they are not tapping into fully – so something must be wrong, there must be a lack. And, if they have been well for a period of time, they go to the doctor and say: 'I am not so sure this is alright,' or, 'Can you check that, please?' It is as if they *want* something to go wrong; they live in constant fear of something going wrong and then do everything to focus on that 'something going wrong' and to manifest it within themselves throughout their lives. The number of check-ups you have that lead to illness; the number of diagnoses that are put upon you by doctors that are incorrect ...but *which give you the illnesses nevertheless because you believe in them, you invest in them, and you therefore create them.*

Many human beings fear lack of finances; they fear lack of health; they fear lack of love. This is a key theme in this chapter today and the one before it – a *lack of Love.* You see so many people wandering through their lives like zombies; people who, from cradle to grave, repeatedly say: 'I do not have enough love. Nobody loves me. People shun me. People don't like me. People ignore me. In any relationship – be it a friendship relationship or a lifetime relationship – I miss out. I don't get enough love.'

Ladies and Gentlemen, *before you can receive Love you have to learn how to give it*, and so few of you know how to give out Love. You are so frightened that there won't be enough *for you* that you find it difficult to give Love first to anyone else. The most contented people on your Earth are those who work tirelessly for others, because, in doing so, they become *complete*. They find that their actions somehow bring them completeness – they feel fulfilled. A lack of Love is a lack of fulfilment and the reason that many people don't feel fulfilled is because they will not reach out in Love to others.

The 'lacks' you feel – the perceived lack of finance, perceived lack of health, perceived lack of Love – *are all expressions of your subconscious belief that you are separated from God.* When you incarnated there was a 'mist', a thick fog placed between you and God's Love – not by God but by yourself and The Field of consciousness you were born into.

This was not meant to be. This happened during The Fall. As a result of the shift of vibrations at that time, the pre-Fall 'light mist' placed around each incarnated soul, and which was simply intended to delineate the 'God as a Whole' from the 'God as the individual' became thicker, became denser, and the energy flow from 'God the

Whole' to 'God the individual' became more difficult for 'God the individual' to pick up, to appreciate, to understand, to take advantage of. At the heart of mankind, at the heart of each soul, is the fear that it has somehow become separated from God. This is not a truth but a *belief* and there have to be certain changes in place before the individuals of *future generations* can interact with God more effectively and be aware of their existence also being one with the Whole. But at present that awareness is not there because of the effects of The Fall, because of the actions of incarnate souls in ancient, ancient times that led to a *believed separation from God*.

When you feel that you lack finances you are in reality feeling that you lack the infinite abundance of God ...and that is a nonsense because *God is you* and through your link with Him He feeds your body with energies, feeds your life at every twist and turn so that you are looked after. I tell you, the beggars and the people on the streets live as beggars and people on the streets because they *have chosen* to do so. They are not to be pitied for the reasons that you normally pity them. They are to be pitied because they have *chosen* that position and do not know that that is what they have done.

God is saying to you: 'Choose Me – don't choose poverty; don't choose fear of a lack of finances on a daily basis. Believe in My ability to do so and will give you fruit, I will give you abundance, I will give you wholeness.'

Your fear of lack of finances is a fear of lack of the Love of God. Your fear of health is a fear (on a subconscious level, going back to The Fall) that God will not provide the energies that your body needs in order to be healthy. But you are part of God; if God is perfect and perfectly healthy then so are you. It is only the perceived separation that gives you this fear, that makes you believe on a soul-level that God will not sustain you. This fear and fear of lack are symptoms of the same core belief.

God constantly sustains you. It is only when you strengthen – thicken – that illusion of separation that you have created between Him and you that you become ill. You thicken the fog so that your soul's understanding of how the energies that flow to you constantly as a gift from God operate is lost in that fog. God's abundant, health giving energies do then not flow into and through you as they should because *you* have prevented them from doing so by your beliefs. Did I not say in the first book that you make yourselves ill? You do! And this is how you do it: you do it by thickening the fog that separates you from God's Love and yet, as I have said, there are many paradoxes in life – that barrier only exists as a perception, a belief, within your subconscious. It is not *actually* there.

So your fear of lack of health is, at source, the same fear as your fear of lack of finances. Your fear of not being loved by others is, at source, also the same fear, because you want God's Love and believe you haven't got it. You have thickened the fog between yourself and God (a barrier which originated all those years ago. This is 'original sin'; this is where it goes back to: *the original sin was to take yourself away from God in consciousness and in sub-consciousness)* and so you feel that there is not enough Love.

God is delivering a deep but simple message to His children to bring them back into the fold and the message has been given to you by many prophets. The message has been given to you by many enlightened souls over the centuries but you do not listen to it. Why should my message, at this stage, be any different than the message of other seers and prophets? It is the same message because it comes from God and it is this: *What you want, you must first give away.*

In giving it away you re-unite yourself with the Whole. Do you see that? If you feel you have a lack of finances, then by giving out finances to someone you re-unite yourself with the whole of mankind. You re-establish your belief at soul-level that you are part of God and that God is abundance and, in doing so, you allow His abundant energies to flow through that fog. Maybe only for today, but if you give again tomorrow they will flow back through that fog tomorrow, and so on, and so on, until you build up a belief that God will always supply to you what you give away, and in greater abundance. When you are giving to Him via His children, He gives back to you with interest – that is Divine law.

You are afraid of illness? Then you have to give your worries about illness over to God. You have to say: 'I am perfect because God is perfect, I release those worries.' In releasing them you make the fog and mist between you and God *thinner* and His healing energies flow to you more readily. Remember, these energies are not being prevented from getting to you by God, they are being blocked by you as a soul because of the perceived barrier that you have inherited as a belief from generations going back to the time of The Fall. So, in releasing your perceptions of illness and saying: 'They don't matter, they're not here, take them away, Father' you allow God's energies to flow more strongly in you and you become healthier.

There are very few human beings on Earth who are as healthy as they should be. Ultimately when that barrier of belief in separation is taken away (by the change that is coming in global perception) people will be super-healthy. They will exist on Earth for far longer in the individual frame than they do at the moment and they will die *happy* (There is an amusing phrase: they will die happy!) because they will not die in pain, they will simply exit this world at the point that is pre-destined for them to do so.

If you want Love you must give Love out. In saying, 'I don't have Love,' you strengthen the barrier around you; you isolate yourself. You must work to see the Love that you want in your own life manifesting in the lives of others – in the people that you meet daily, in the people that you talk to on your telephones, at work, everywhere. As an exercise, as you are watching the news look at the people in the news stories and send your Love out to them. In sending your Love out to them (which at first will, to many of you, seem like an *alien* thing to do) you begin to tear down the barrier.

Love is a flow of energy. Energy, by its nature, has to flow. Abundance is an incoming and an outpouring of energy. Health is an incoming and an outpouring of energy. Love is an incoming and an outpouring flow of energy and *you have to re-connect to that flow*. Everything in God's universe operates by 'give and take'; by a sending out and a drawing in – but you have to send out before you can draw in and the joy is: as you send out you draw in *automatically* because God feeds you. I have to stress that at no time is God making a judgement in any of His donations of energy to you. His energy, His fulfillment, His Love, His abundance, His health are *always* there for you – they are with you and in you now. It is *you* who is making a judgement and saying: 'I'm not worthy of these things; I don't have these things; I need to worry about these things,' and all the time you build that barrier between you and God's sustaining and healing Light.

God is constantly knocking at the door of your soul and saying: 'Here I am – here are the things that you need. You can have them. They are yours. You do not need to take them from anyone else.' But you think you do.

You think you do!

The most important perceived lack is the lack of security. This is why you fight each other; why you kill each other, because you feel that your way is going to be undermined by someone else: 'This is all I have. If someone changes the way that I feel or think, how will I exist?' Lack of security! ...In religion – lack of security! ...In politics – lack of security!

It is only when you tear down the internal barriers that you rediscover the security of being a part of God.

What have you to fear? You cannot be ill. You cannot be poor. You cannot be unloved. You are not going to die. You inherit the Kingdom. You are a child of God. What have you to fear – *only the barrier that you have erected*.

Oh, if only I could now, in talking to you (and putting this down eventually into book-form), reach into the *hearts* of the terrorists and the murderers and the dictators and those who commit domestic violence, those who commit violence against children; reach into their hearts and say: 'You are doing this out of fear – for no other reason. Let go of your fear – let the God-Energy in and you will stop what you are doing.'

I see many children on this side who come over bruised and abused and who need very careful attention in order to forget their wounds and to grow back into the souls that they really are. I see many people who come over to my side of life – to the entry levels of my side of life – who have been killed in various violent, terrible, terrible ways and there is no need for any of it. There is no need for disunity. You see what The Fall did to you: it not only separated you from God but it separated you from *each other*. The fog that you have around you – the perceived barrier – prevents you from loving, prevents you from sharing, from understanding harmony: the peace and love of knowing that you are part of each other and that you can never be alone.

At this point in your existence you have to wait until you get to the spirit levels of life before you can experience that in *even* a small way. And the concept of group souls that act as one organism (yet are composed of individuals) must seem very strange to you, but it is such a loving way of life, such a comfortable existence where there is no stress, no longer any lack.

I want to see each of you reading this book being rich, being loved, being fulfilled and wanting for nothing. There is no magic formula that the illusions of The Field of consciousness of mankind can give you that will enable you to be this way. There is only the God that you must turn to. You must give out, give away those things you want in order to receive them from God; you must let go of your perceptions of negativity to provoke a high energy response from God; you must let go of your perceptions of lack in order to find abundance; embrace and give out your ability to Love in order to be Loved – and all these things are then yours forever.

As you are at the moment you deliver only trouble to, and therefore request only trouble from, God. Does that shock you?

Let me explain – God experiences, knows of, your troubles, but in the way of a neutral observer, not attributing to them the gravity and the emotion and the misery that you do. He experiences them because He cannot do otherwise. They do not shake Him or sway Him or depress Him or diminish Him but they are known to Him because He experiences unique aspects of His Creation through each of you – that was your original purpose in wearing the illusive veil of individuality and of setting out into the physical universe – to bring further experience, through your adventures in that physical universe, to God.

You therefore present to God all your experiences in life... you present Him with trouble when you are troubled. You present Him with pain when you are in pain. You present Him with worry when you are worried. You offer all your experiences to Him, share all your experiences with Him. Whether you are aware of it or not, you are an energy conduit constantly bringing information to Him. What you do not understood is that the information you bring to Him as a result of your subconscious beliefs attracts – brings back – harmonious energies; that is, energies of a similar frequency, of the same kind, *to you*. What you do not understood is that the experiences you bring to God carry with them a 'request' for more of the same energy to be given back to you from Him to support – to maintain – the inner and outer illusions of the negative, difficult experiences you are having, until such time as you modify them. God constantly supplies your subconscious demands; he supplies to you more of what you demand from Him on a subconscious level, on a level of belief. Therefore, if your energy demands through your beliefs are for more poverty, for more lack, then those beliefs are reinforced by the energy that flows back to you from the Godhead. You subconsciously and constantly request more of the same because like attracts like.

You shout out to God and say: 'My God, why have you abandoned me?' He has not. Quite the opposite. He has supplied your demands perfectly and exactly. God's energies are supplied to you constantly at the level of your subconscious request for more of the same vibrations you believe to be dominant in your life. You also contribute to and draw energies from The Field of mankind, which reinforces your belief in it daily by supplying to you more of what you believe to be true in the world you see around you and feel within you.

…Do you now begin to understand that, as God functions, so do you? You are made in His image in your ability to mould and shape matter and concepts. You deliver to and draw energies from the Godhead; you also deliver to and draw energies from The Field.

God wishes the best for his children. He wishes to bring you His fulfilment and abundance, but He can only supply according to your demand because He has given you complete freedom of choice. You choose what it is that you want from Him, and also what you want from The Field, through your subconscious and conscious beliefs. You therefore have to let go of your belief in lack, your belief that The Field is delivering lack to you on a daily basis, and you have to let God's Light energies flow into you, and through you into The Field, allowing those energies from the heart of God (which are perfect and positive and harmonious) to reaffirm and re-establish your identity and power as a soul in your thinking, in your actions, in your physicality, in your ability to shape and change the 'reality' of The Field around you.

(*Michael: Joseph*'s lecture ends at this point with a small piece of information for our group on the production of a book detailing exactly what happened in The Fall.)

I have referred again to The Fall today and I wish you to know that we are working on that book; that we are working on an extensive account of The Fall for you so that you can reference it in the other books, in my books and in other books that you will put out in the future.

Chapter 6

Neutralising your fears and temptations

Joseph speaks. Today's chapter concerns something that you do not understand at all in your daily lives and that is fear and temptation and the consequences of fear and temptation.

You are creators; each of you is part of God and has God-Powers within you – the power to create, as I have said in the past, a paradise or a hell for yourselves. And this you do at an individual level and at a global level. But you are unaware of the power of your thoughts and of your ability to 'breathe life' into them. It is said that *God breathed life into man* in your Biblical story; God actually breathed out and positioned you in your own illusion of individuality. That is the fact. He did not take clay and make a man; He created an illusion of separation for you so that you could experience and then return to Him with the 'jewels', the treasure of that experience, to add to the Whole.

You cannot stop being God!

That is a very important sentence – *you cannot stop being God*. In other words, whether you are aware of it or not, whether you deny it or not, you function *every second* of your life on Earth as God and so, in microcosm, you create as God creates. You have all of God's attributes. How could you not have God's attributes if you are a part of the Whole? You are able to channel those attributes daily whether you are aware of that or not. And the sceptics and the atheists and those who push God out entirely *still work as God* because it is only their physical minds that separate them from being part of the Whole. They cannot be separated at soul-level and so they bring forth Creation whether they are aware of it or not, whether they acknowledge it or not. *They are part of God despite what they believe!* Belief has nothing to do with the reality of being part of the Whole.

The mind is a filter, it is a projector, and so the soul, minute to minute, imagines, dreams, creates and pushes its creative intents, wishes, through the matrix of the mind, through the projector, and it is the projector that turns those wishes (whether those wishes are conscious or sub-conscious) into form.

Mankind fears many things: it can fear high places; it can fear low places; it can fear pain; it can fear loss; it fears death; it fears life in many ways. It, therefore, pushes into the matrix of the mind a concept of that fear, an embodiment of that fear, and that embodiment is then given life and attached to the human soul. So the soul externalises its fears through the matrix of the mind and the fears then become (because the soul is a creator, is God) mobile, become tangible, become an unseen irritant within the sphere of the aura of the soul.

The soul is constantly creating and feeding its own fears. Those fears then are given enough power by the soul to work on the soul *to the detriment of that soul.*

The soul constantly carries around its own fears and its fears are there to 'tempt' it. *What it fears it gives strength to.* What your soul fears it gives strength to, because it is constantly feeding that fear with life-force energy to create the fear. This is why in many cultures we say: 'What you resist, persists', because what you resist you give strength to. To combat fear you erect a barrier rather than affirming that there is nothing there at all. You say, 'I push out that fear. I put up a barrier between myself and that fear,' thus acknowledging that there *is* a fear and thus giving strength to the fear and making it stronger.

You cannot *fight* any 'temptation' (i.e. anything that you fear, anything that gives you doubt) by resisting it. In resisting it you give it form. What you have to do instead is completely take your mind off the fear; not to say, 'There is no such fear,' (because in saying that you are acknowledging that there *is* a fear) but to take your mind off it completely, to offer no resistance to anything that you fear. ...In a way to 'welcome' it, because in welcoming a fear, in embracing it, in putting your arms around it, in loving it, you take it back into your soul and the higher molecules of Creation then absorb it and transmute it and get rid of it for you.

You may wonder why I am talking about temptations; why this would be relevant in a book that is a constructive book to help you change your world. I have to tell you this because you have to acknowledge that *you are the creator of the things that you fear.* In acknowledging that you fear things you draw them towards yourself. You do this globally by saying, 'This person is different than I am, therefore this person is something to be feared.' By saying, 'This person is different,' *they become different*; by saying, 'This person is someone to be feared,' *they become someone to be feared.*

You create you own enemies.

Isn't that a revolutionary thought? *You create your own enemies* by making the people you fear into what you fear; by making them (in your own mind and externally) into the stereotypes you have created of them. This is why such wisdom came from Jesus, why such wisdom came from the prophets: *Love your enemies.* If you Love your enemies they are no longer your enemies because you change your perception of them and they react to you based on the vibrations that you are giving out to them.

Wars are caused by temptation. Violence is caused by temptation because, unseen around you, around every person, around every nation, there are thought-forms; there are entities that you have created that are an embodiment of your own fears, your own perversions, your own angers, and you draw these forms towards you at times when you are investing in negative emotions, in negative thoughts. When a person becomes angry… if a person is angry at their wife, or their husband, or their own children… crackling around the energy that they have produced are other like-energies that reinforce that anger and 'tempt' that person into becoming more angry.

How often have you come down from a position of anger and thought: 'How could I be like that? What has made me so angry? Why did I want to sustain the anger? Why did I want to go beyond my own anger and become more and more violent, more and more outraged, more and more indignant? Why did I say things that I didn't want to say? And why, from this position of relative calm now, does my episode of anger seem like another person talking and not myself?' It is because in moments of anger you activate, you bring towards yourselves, those thought-forms that vibrate at the same frequency and add to your anger. It is in the interests of those thought-forms (because you have given them a degree of 'awareness'- though not an awareness in the sense of the soul's awareness – 'need' is a better word… you have given them a *need*) to stimulate your lower emotional responses so that you feed them with energy.

Be still is something else you have been told by the prophets, by the elevated spirits who have come to visit you over the millennia, over the years. Be still because, in being still, you allow the higher vibrations of your soul, of your heart, to activate and you push away the thought-forms that are around you. You do not activate them, you do not feed them with your own energy.

Be still!

Look from within, but not from within the mind.

The mind exists to serve, although it is the dominating factor in most human beings. The mind feeds through its matrix – puts out – creative molecules based on what it feels the soul is instructing it to do. So, in times of anger, the mind is instructed by the soul that is angry (and not thinking straight) to feed that anger out to the aspects of anger – the entities – that the soul has created around itself and thus give them more power. Your mind is instructed to be the irritant that it often is *by your soul*. The soul on Earth, feeling that it needs guidance, seeks that guidance not from itself, not from its heart centre that connects it, that is a *direct telephone line to God*, but from the mind, a mind it has programmed to create and to attract fear.

The mind, because the soul is uncertain, feeds back uncertainty to the soul, and this is why the mind *irritates* so many people. This is why it seems to be dominant, because it has been given domination over the soul as a result of constant requests for guidance from the soul. The soul seeks solace from the mind but the mind is only a matrix, a filter between the soul and the illusion that you are living in. And the mind is only operating under the soul's instructions when it gives you such a difficult time.

You have to take power back from the mind in order to be peaceful; you have to re-seat your power into your heart. You have to look from within and, in times of anger and in times of discord, you have to say to yourself: 'I will stop this now,' and in doing so the mind stops pouring out more power into the thought-forms that you have created. Anger is a vicious circle. Fear is a vicious circle. I hope I am explaining this clearly. It should explain to you who are reading this book why there are such fanatics on your world, why there are such prejudiced people. Their fanaticisms, their prejudices and their perversions stem from fear and in fearing something you create it – you give it power.

Many of your religions are, unfortunately, based on fear, fear of those who are not like you, and are nothing to do with God. In fearing those who are not like you, you build them up; you make them into what you fear, which begs the question: *do people react to you based on your perception of them* and, yes, they do!

So you are not blameless in any situation globally because you contribute to it by your perception of it, because you feed energy into it, through the matrix of your mind, dependent on your dominant beliefs.

If you would change this world (and this is what this book is about), you have to first recognise that your fears, your angers and your prejudices have power and that *you* have given them that power. You have created little 'devils', if you will, because of your own dominant thoughts. In recognising this you take your power back and you can step back from the daily dramas you enter into and say: 'I am not doing this. Wait a moment, I am becoming angry. Why? I am God – God is not angry, therefore I am not angry. I stop the words I am going to say. I stop the thoughts I am about to think and I become calm and I think of something peaceful and loving. If I find myself being angry towards someone (no matter what I perceive them to have done or to be doing against me) I stop my perception of what is happening and I send Love out to that person. If I cannot send Love out to that person, I withdraw from the situation. I refuse to argue. I refuse to feed the fear and to feed their fears.' Remember, just as there are entities around you that you have created, there are entities around other people that vibrate at a similar rate. Fear has a certain frequency; anger has a certain frequency, and once you tap into that frequency you bring towards yourself not only your own fears that are nested around you, but the fears of other people too.

Is it any wonder that there are such wars and such violence across the globe?

Why should this be? Why should you be capable of creating negative things as well as positive things? Because you are God and because your perception is wrong – because you are lost in the mists of the illusion, but help is always close – the God within is constantly saying to you, 'Always remember – be still and I will guide you.'

There has to be a change. You will never win a war. No-one ever wins a war; no-one ever wins a conflict. Conflicts are eruptions of violent energy, nothing more. No-one has ever won a war! No-one has ever, on a governmental level or a military level, installed peace, brought peace to a nation. What happens is that the violence feeds and feeds itself until it can feed itself no longer; until people's thoughts weary of violence. They restore peace to themselves through a longing inside that is put out through the matrix of the mind and peace is then created.

No-one wins a war, no-one wins in violence, no-one wins in an angry moment; no-one wins in an argument. You cannot win – you are fighting yourself.

You are fighting yourself!

Anger is a temptation from outside… but you have created it. Perversions are a temptation from outside… but you have created them. And if you are sensitive enough then you will feel, hear, almost *taste* the temptations of the world because they are vibrating at a frequency that you can sense. If you are spiritually aware then you can sense a whole spectrum, a waveband, of different emotions.

So, to the spiritually aware I have to say, those times when you feel violence and think it is you *it is not*. And for those who are angry as they read this book – angry people – if you lose your temper, if you are prejudiced, if you are angry towards certain factions of humanity – stop. Stop now! To make a difference – stop! If you cannot become loving instantly then become *neutral*, and in being neutral (when you put your cars into neutral gear they cannot go anywhere), if you put your desires into neutral, then the mind is stalled, the mind is in neutral: it is not putting out any contributions negatively to what is happening in your world.

This has been a rather long and involved topic but I want you to be aware of your potential to create. Even a child, even a baby, creates its fears around it; externalises its fears through the vehicle of its mind. And, at any time, any one of you has fears in passive state waiting to be re-activated by the mind.

At this stage in your evolution it is enough that you quiet those aspects of yourself – those fears that you have created and have given a degree of awareness to. At a later stage in your evolution you will stop creating them. That is God's plan: for you to stop creating them. All this goes back to you getting it wrong many years ago. I keep referring to The Fall, and I have to, because at the time of The Fall you decided to create a mini-universe, if you like. You distanced yourselves from God through the change of vibration that occurred in The Fall and you created 'demons' and you created fears. You created things that were not present before The Fall, before you became anxious and wanted to do things your way (not realising that the 'your way' you were thinking about came from the physical mind and not the soul, because there is only your way, there is only God's way and you are God). Through that distancing came negativity, came fear, came demons, came entities; and there are still those souls who 'lurk' (I suppose is the word) in human form, who are deeply perverted by the illusion that goes back to The Fall.

There are still those who require negative energy, who revel in negative energy, who absorb the energies of fear and anger – as do the entities that are around you. It is these souls that are the *most lost* in the illusion and the *most dangerous* in the illusion. And, because of God's plan for all souls, you cannot abandon them. They will never be abandoned; they have to come back to the Light. They cannot forever and for infinity be surrounded by an illusion of power and an illusion of the need for anger and fear – those things are not of God. *God has to retrieve all His children* because He cannot lose a part of Himself; He cannot sever a part of Himself from the Whole. So these souls one day have to come back into the fold.

There have been many of them over the years: those that incite racial hatred, those that incite war, those that suppress, oppress and eliminate other souls. These are the perpetrators, originally, of The Fall and they need your help! They need your Love because, in loving them, you *neutralise* them. But you need to Love them as a global response – you need hundreds, thousands, millions of souls to Love them into silence, to Love them into neutrality, to put to sleep their negative response to the illusion. And then at that stage they can be reached by their angelic counterparts, who are constantly trying to bring them back to the correct vision of who they are and to make them recognise their heritage; recognise that they are lost souls and must change, must come back into the fold, must migrate back to God.

Today's chapter has been about dark things, dark aspects of yourselves, but only in understanding the darkness can you see the Light and the power of the Light. I am trying to give you 'weapons' for the future: weapons that kill no-one, weapons that destroy nothing, but weapons that are potent in ending war ...and fear ...and anger ...and perversion.

Also consider that, whilst your entities may not be strong enough to permanently overwhelm you (and they are not: there are times when you are angry, there are times when you are peaceful) they can *and do* influence weaker souls. So the person with the smoking gun who says, 'Someone told me to do it,' is not lying. The predators of life who feed on the weak and the lonely and the children are acting, yes, on their own desires, but also on their own desires fuelled by the power of entities who can get through to them, who can influence them.

What I am saying to you is that *we are all personally responsible.*

That sentence may seem abhorrent to you. 'I am nothing to do with the perverts,' you will say. 'I am nothing to do with the violent. I am nothing to do with the angry. I am nothing to do with those people who have caused so much pain in life.' *Yes, you are,* because you are linked to them, because you make available to them (through your own angers and fears) *voices* that can influence them, that can feed their need to be violent, to be angry, to be perverted.

There is no criticism intended in telling you this but it is a sobering thought and it shows you the need for 'the neutral way', the need not to put anger and fear and thoughts of unrest into this world, and to check yourself first before you criticise anyone else; to neutralise your own demons, your own nightmares. And you do this by recognising when you are about to spark off such bursts of energy that put power into your own entities and into the world and by saying: 'Stop!'

Be evolved enough to stop; be spiritual enough to stop.

Many of your holy men and women seek solitude and they are wise to seek solitude because it is easier to be focused, to be strong and not to be tempted when you are in a position of solitude. But that is a short-term solution. There are too many aspects of God for each of you to be in solitude *physically* but you can be in solitude *spiritually* through meditation. You can enter into the chamber of your soul and review how you are acting on a daily basis and, if there is something that you wish to change, then change it. Don't look to psychiatrists ...and doctors ...and lawyers ...and military men ...and politicians to change how you are. It is nothing to do with them; it is to do with you. Peace starts with you. Harmony starts with you. The way home for those lost souls (yourself included to a degree) starts with you.

You are all tempted; you are all urged to be violent by the cloud of vibration that you have created around yourselves over countless ages.

But you can change now as you read this. You *will* change now if you put into practice what I have suggested. Neutrality first, then spirituality, peace, harmony – it lies with you.

(*Michael: Joseph* concludes this lecture with more encouragement for our group regarding the putting out into the world of **Revelation: Joseph's Message**. Again, it is included here because it contains valuable information for all.)

Joseph. Before I leave today (although that is a relative term), many [here] have voiced their appreciation of the book being created (**Revelation: Joseph's Message**). I must add my voice and say that it is wonderful to see a representation of what we have spoken about – all of us together (*a reference to the others in the soul-group*) – being available to other souls. And, further to what I have been saying today, you must remove from that book all fears of it not being huge. You must acknowledge it as being huge, as being a *salvation* for people. That is not a big-headed thing to say. The book contains wisdom and you would be amazed at how many souls have been involved in its creation, as they are involved in the creation of this second volume.

And we wish you to know that we are with you in your difficult times; in the times when the Earth pulls at you; in the times when you do not know what you are doing or how to go forward, or how to think, or how to stop thinking. We are with you. We want you to know that and we can help as much as you will allow us to help because we have been given permission to do so.

Thank God each day for the book finding new avenues and be brave, because you will be asked to do magnificent things in its name; to champion its cause; to travel on its behalf; to talk to people, to persuade them, to encourage them. Be brave. There is a great deal of work to do.

Chapter 7

You possess the ultimate super-weapon

Joseph speaks. Good morning. This chapter is about 'weapons'. You make much of weapons in your society; you believe them to be defence; you believe that if you have 'might' then you cannot be conquered, that you are secure and, should anyone try to invade your territory (or your heart, on an emotional level) *they will be dealt with*.

Conventional weapons will never solve the problems of the world, no matter how many you stockpile, no matter who has the most, because there is always the potential that those weapons will be *used*. Conventional weapons always cause damage to *someone*. Some may survive, yes, but in order for someone to survive, someone else must die or be maimed.

I wish to introduce you today to a different weapon; to a weapon that *does* change your life, *will* change your world and keeps you safer than any conventional weapon ever could.

That weapon is Light.

Of course it is Light – what else would I say? But you have to learn as individuals and as nations and groups how to use Light, God-Light, because Light can be *directed*.

First of all, the nature of God-Light is to *cleanse* on the lower levels of vibration. Wherever there is a situation that involves heavy vibration – negative thoughts and negative actions – God-Light cleanses, chases away, replaces that vibration with a higher vibration. And within that higher vibration of God-Light no evil, no negativity, no violence, no perversion can exist.

The thought-molecules, if you will, of the negative field of mankind cannot exist in a higher field of vibration. This is why you have such problems in communicating with us. Most human beings, unfortunately, exist within the greater field of the illusion but also within personal fields that are tainted by negative vibrations. Which of you at times is not sad, or depressed, or angry, or ill, or resenting, or bitter? And, if you say: 'That is not me,' then you should not be reading this book! Each of you on Earth suffers (to a lesser or greater degree) from the effects of negative vibrations, and in doing so you place around yourself and within your aura a wall that, from your point of view, separates you from higher visions, from communicating with us, from seeing us on a regular basis. It also prevents you from having higher thoughts because your thoughts resonate at the same vibration, usually, as the dominant vibrations within your aura.

So, if you are a person with a dominance of negative vibration (a dominance of sadness, or anger, etc.) then your thoughts will resonate at that same level and will separate you from God. God has not separated you from Himself; you have separated yourself from Him by the nature of your vibrations. So in all cases, whether a person is ill, whether a person is violent, whether a person is perverted, whether a person is bitter and unforgiving, whether a person is vindictive – in all these cases what is missing from their aura and from their minds and from their hearts is God-Light. God-Light knows nothing of these lower vibrations.

So the weapon I am suggesting you use is Light and the reason I am suggesting you use it is that it purges from people (when properly used) the negative vibrations that they have accumulated during their lifetimes.

How do you use Light as a weapon? You will need to use your imaginations. Each of you has been given an imagination, an ability to create. In order to create you first need to *visualise*; you visualise and you then bring into being that which you have visualised.

If you are reading this and saying, 'I don't have an imagination,'- *nonsense*, of course you do! It is simply that certain human beings seem to wear their imagination, their creative ability, closer to the surface – and therefore be more consciously aware of it – than others. But each of you can dream. Each of you dreams, do you not, at night? Each of you has an imaginative capacity, a creative capacity. You need to use that capacity in order to wield the weapon of Light.

A Meditation.

> To wield the weapon of Light you first of all need a quite time. There is always a need for quiet on your Earth; always a need for silence… *You need a quiet time.*
>
> You need to set aside time to *deploy* your weapon.
>
> During that quiet time you then, in your imagination, see souls and situations that you wish to change: the group of people that does not behave as you think it should; the group that is perhaps more violent than it should be; the individuals you wish would change so that they stop harming other human beings; the heads of state and heads of government that are responsible for policies that cause harm to people; the national thinking from certain centres around your globe (including your own) that leads to despondency, that leads to upset for human beings. You see

– visualise – these things in your mind's eye and then you bring your weapon of Light to bear.

In the case of an individual, see that individual standing in front of you (and you will have to be brave and loving at this point because you will have to discard all judgements on that person, all your personal biases, the revulsion you perhaps feel at times towards them. All these things you must put aside). Visualise streaming through you, coming down from the top of your head and out through your solar plexus towards that person, a stream of perfect white Light – brilliant white Light – which you then see surrounding the person. It will help sometimes to perhaps see the person dressed in grey and to then see, as the Light hits them, the Light turning that grey into white. See them as being immersed in that white Light to the extent that you cannot see their outline any longer – all you can see is the white Light. Then leave that Light with them as you drop your connection to that person with a: 'God bless you, you are held in God-Light this day.'

You can then move on to greater assemblies of souls; you can move on to larger groups of people and the places they live. Picture in your mind the shape of the region of the world that you are sending Light out to. Again, do not judge, but instead send Light into the outline of that region – seeing every man, woman and child being bathed in the white Light. See them disappear into the white Light, see the location disappear into the white Light and then move on with a: 'God bless you, you are held in God-Light this day.'

This weapon can be used for individuals, groups, heads of state and governments as I have said, but it can also be used as a tremendous force for healing. The people who suffer from terminal illnesses, the people who suffer from constant pain and from defects in their bodies are doing so for a variety of reasons – some of which are karmic – but many of which are because they have gathered around themselves so much negativity that that Light they sorely need is prevented from getting to them from within themselves. (In the normal course of things there should be no illness as I have explained in the past.) In cases like these you also have the opinions of the people who surround those who are ill to contend with, because their husbands and wives and bothers and sisters and relatives and friends, and the medical profession *all* believe, in their heart-of-hearts, that the person is seriously or terminally ill. So they contribute to the wall of negativity that prevents the Light getting to the patient. You have to combat that!

If you know someone who is terminally ill, who is suffering greatly physically or mentally, picture them in front of you. See them in perhaps in a dark grey and, as you send the Light out to them – drawing it in through your head chakra and pouring it out through your solar plexus – then see that dark-grey turning to light-grey, the light-grey turning to cream, the cream turning to white and then them disappearing into the God-Light. Confirm for them: 'This day you are healthy. You are filled with God-Light. Amen.' and move on in your mind to the next case or gently come out of your meditation.

(*Michael:* at this point, as you end your meditation, please remember to ask God to protect you and to guide you and to close your chakras for you as explained in Chapter 4.)

Remember that God does not place barriers between Himself and His children but His children produce barriers that shut Him out.

Light is needed on your level of consciousness on a daily basis. As I have said before you will never change the world with ideals, you will never change the world through weaponry, you will never change the world with war. You are perpetuating the negativity that keeps you *trapped* in this level of the illusion. You have to change the world through changing perception; by allowing people to *see* clearly, and at the moment they do not see clearly; they see through the glass *darkly* because they have surrounded themselves with so much negativity.

Your mission is to restore to people what is theirs by heritage, by Divine heritage. Remember that each of you is an angel, each of you is an angel encapsulated in dark matter, in heavy vibrations, because of the effects of the change that occurred millennia ago.

I wish to talk for a little while about the effects of Light on seemingly solid objects as well, about the effects of Light on the Earth itself, because the Earth is being strangled by The Field at the moment.

The Earth is dying.

The Earth is dying and the pollution that you see and the cataclysms that you see are the end result of thoughts that have been put into the Earth years ago. The Earth requires Light because, as you spread across the Earth as incarnate souls after The Fall you bathed the Earth not in Light but in your own vibrations of darkness, of worry, of loss, of fear, of separation from God. You blanket the Earth – you cover the Earth – with your presence and with your thoughts and, by doing so, you shut out from the Earth the God-Light that *it too* needs to regenerate.

So, as an exercise I would like you to take an object from your house that perhaps is not very precious to you, an everyday object (it can be a cup, it can be an ornament or it can be a stuffed toy – something that you really don't care one way or another for). Place that object in front of you in your meditations and send Light into it in the same way that

I have taught you to send Light into people. Do this for a week and then hold the object and see how you feel about it and you will see that Love now emanates from that object. No matter what it looks like physically, it will have Love within it and you will feel that that object is special to you and should have a special place within your home. You have transmuted the molecules of that object to a higher vibration of reality by dowsing it in spiritual Light.

And you can do this with the Earth; you can do this with a tree, with a plant, with a field, with a house, with a mountain, with a stream.

Each of you reading this book is capable of changing this Earth because you can hold the whole Earth in front of you in your meditation and pour Light into it – just as I have told you to do with individuals and with groups. In your mind's eye you can see the Earth at first as being polluted and then pour Light into it so that it becomes lighter and lighter in colour until it is immersed in and disappears into the white Light ...and you will have changed the Earth.

If enough of you do this (and many, *many* of you *need to* do this) you will bring new life, new nourishment, to this planet and the planet will re-energise without having to go through a series of cataclysms to rid itself of the human condition in order for it to do so.

This is the alternative: if *you* kill off the Earth (and God will not do it – *you* will do it as a species) then the Earth will move into a fallow period and will be cleared by angels, by angelic forces, and prepared again for the human spirit to inhabit it.

These are the two choices you have:

Do something.

Or do nothing and the Earth will die.

...*There* is a stark warning for you.

You are able to transmute matter because you are part of God. Therefore, it is time for *each of you* reading this book (and as many of your friends and as many of your relatives as you can convince to absorb this knowledge) to begin to change things – not politically but spiritually; not through violence but by the way of God. Changing things – this is what this book is about.

How can you change this Earth? I have told you how to do it. You will put barriers up; you will say, 'Joseph, I don't believe that this can work. I have had no evidence that this can work.' Don't just use your physical eyes and your physical senses – in the name of God I tell you that this works and you will prove it to yourself gradually: ...through the person who is miraculously cured of their illness and no-one knows why ...through the situation that you diffuse by sending Light into it and you will think, 'I never thought that such a positive conclusion could come out of it' ...through the objects that you imbue with Love and change them and are then strangely attracted to because of what you have put into them.

It is down to you.

Remember, you have an enemy in your head; you have the physical mind that will always tell you that these things are not possible. The physical mind wants to keep the status quo; it doesn't want you to be free. There is a consciousness, as I have said, to reality (to the illusion that you take to be 'reality') and that consciousness wishes to maintain itself as it is, wishes to feed itself and, unfortunately, it feeds itself through your negative thoughts.

Before I close on this subject I must tell you that it is very important in your households that you keep yourselves buoyant; that you forgive each other; that you fail to rise to petty argument because in petty argument, in resenting each other, you increase the negativity that is within your auras. And you build into your houses – which should be sanctuaries of Light – you build into your household environments darkness, chaos, vibrations of greyness and blackness which attract thought-forms from the lower levels that resonate at a similar vibration to other violent perceptions around your world and draw them to you.

When you argue, Brothers and Sisters, you bring *war* into your house. When you hate each other and are angry with each other, you bring similar vibrations from around your globe into your auras and into your homes. You identify with the very things that you say are so terrible in the news. You become a part of them for the duration of your arguments, for the duration of your domestic violence. Have you ever noticed after you have rowed how heavy your houses are; how there seems to be a pressure on your heads; how it takes so long to clear the air? (Believe me, you *need* to clear the air following such mistaken behaviour). No one is perfect... the change in your world will take time but it has to start *now*.

If you find yourself getting angry, forgive yourself and use the same exercise on yourself. Sit down, be quiet, refuse to say anything. See yourself drawing to yourself the Light through the head chakra*. See it not coming out through the solar plexus but instead infusing your own body with Light (and the bodies of those that are close to you). See it transmuting the greyness and the blackness that you have attracted into white Light, and in doing so you will diffuse the situation within yourself, you will get rid of the negativity, you will not attract entities from the lower levels of vibration and you will keep your home a place of white Light.

When you keep your home a place of white Light people like me – my Brothers and Sisters on this level and other levels – find it easier to get through to you; to communicate through your intuition, to give

---

* Michael: your head chakra is an energy vortex located at the crown of your head.

you advice as to how you should live your lives, as to how you can continue building Light into the world and into yourselves.

So, in this Chapter I have introduced you to the ultimate weapon. It is free; it does not demand physical resources. It does not cause suffering.

It is Light and the time to wield it is *now*.

Chapter 8

You can work magic in your life

Michael's notes. This short chapter came as an unexpected 'bonus', in that its recording took place whilst Jane, David and myself were out on an evening walk in a dense wood in the Lake District during a brief holiday for our two families. It followed on from a lecture given to us by another of our guides, '*Silver Star*', for our website*. It was raining heavily at the time, forcing us to take shelter under the trees. I stood rigidly in trance for almost an hour, Jane holding up our recorder and hardly daring to move in case any slight noise broke my trance state, with the result that her hand was badly cramped afterwards. Any fellow tourists passing by would have found us to be a most curious little group... the rain therefore proving to be a blessing as it kept holidaymakers indoors whilst we were receiving this communication!

Joseph speaks. This is a good venue. It would be a great idea if you were to take yourselves away to somewhere quiet to record my lectures. You are *safer* if you can find somewhere away from everyone than you are in a house where there is always the problem of someone knocking on the door, or on the window, or of passing noise, or of some other disturbance. When you *can* get out there is more power and more energy in the countryside and you will be able to work longer than you do indoors – although the room we prepared at

---

* www.michaelandjane.co.uk

Michael and Jane's house in conjunction with you all is a great source of power and we appreciate that, as the weather darkens, you need a roof over your heads in order to work with me.

I would like to speak very briefly...relatively briefly... this evening about *magic*.

Magic and the art of the magician have been around far longer than you appreciate and there were entertainments *even* in my time where illusion was used to thrill people. Magic today seems to have become a very conformed subject with your magicians running through a variety of expected tricks ranging from card tricks to the 'production' of birds to so-called 'levitation', and it is all rather formulaic and quite boring from my point of view.

I wish you to tell the people who read this book that they are each a *magician* capable of performing real magic in their lives and I wish to give them a further meditation this evening to combat fear and the problems of life in conjunction with what my colleague has just been saying. (Michael: *Joseph*'s reference here is to the lecture on fear given at the start of this session by *Silver Star*, which can be found on our website.)

A Meditation.

> When you are under stress, when you are fearful, when you are at a low ebb, when you do not know which way to turn, I would ask you to become very still and to imagine that you are standing on a stage, dressed resplendently in a very fine magician's outfit. Imagine that you are looking out from the lit stage towards the 'audience', but that the 'audience' consists only of empty seats except for *one seat* with a spotlight shining down on it right in the centre of the theatre, and that in that seat sits an image of yourself. That image of yourself represents the problem you are

experiencing and wish to eliminate. The seated image of yourself as you begin your meditation should look unsettled, troubled, fearful because of the particular situation you need to beat, to circumvent, to alleviate.

I want you to imagine, as I have said, that you are on a stage and that the image of yourself on that stage is one of a powerful person, a healthy person, a commanding person, an assured person; that you have control over all elements and circumstances of life that come to you.

I then want you to take from your head the splendid magician's top hat that you are wearing and to hold it in front of you. Now consider, bring to mind, the situation you find yourself in but consider it, review it, 'from a distance': *dispassionately*. You are distanced from it because it is represented by that other person, that image of yourself that is sitting down in the theatre at the centre, not by the empowered image of yourself standing on the stage.

I want you to now reach into that hat using your imagination and to bring out of it not a rabbit (unless you particularly like that image, but if it is a rabbit you choose it should be a rabbit *made out of Light*) but to bring out of the hat a sphere of Light, to hold it in front of you having produced it from the hat and to see it as a beautiful, pulsating sphere of energy that is threaded through with Love, with assurance, with comfort... and with a solution to your problem.

Then you are to see the sphere you are holding reflected in the eyes of the image of yourself that is sitting in the centre of the theatre. Now throw the sphere from your hands towards the other figure of yourself that is sitting out there in front of you.

See the sphere gently floating across to the other you. As the sphere touches the other you it strikes the heart centre of the other you and begins to be absorbed by your other self. The glow from the sphere expands from the heart centre until the other you is completely enclosed in a bubble of brilliant white Light. As you observe the other you from the stage, as you look at this image of yourself, you can see the expression on their – *your* – face *change – lighten* – as they are presented with the solution to their, to *your*, problem.

Reach into the top hat again and draw out a second sphere of Light and throw that new sphere towards the other you in the seat and see the same process take place until the other you is surrounded by an even more brilliant white Light. Repeat the exercise as many times as you wish to, seeing each new sphere increasing, intensifying the amount of Light in the bubble containing the other you.

Know then that within that white Light the solution to your problem, the 'magic' that you need, has been presented to you, has entered you through your heart centre, is being absorbed via your chakras, is within your aura and is manifest *now*. Know that God, the God that surrounds you and the God that is within you – *is* you – has provided the answer and the solution to your problem. Realise that you no longer need to worry about it, that the solution is within you and will shortly make itself manifest in your life.

Now bow to your other self silently and with Love. See the theatre curtains come down from either side of the stage to meet in front of you, and slowly and calmly return to your physical existence.

(*Michael:* sorry to repeat myself but this is important until it becomes second nature to you: as you end your meditation, remember to ask God to protect you and to guide you and to close your chakras for you as explained in Chapter 4.)

…You might say, 'Joseph, if I have a solution in mind to my problem, why can't I use it in this meditation?' Ah! You may have solutions 'in mind' but do you have solutions 'in heart'? Is the solution in your mind the right solution for you? If it is not then no amount of drawing it out of the top hat will make it happen for you.

In bringing out pure Light, pure *magic*, within which anything and everything is possible, you surround yourself, you penetrate your heart centre, with the vibrations that are necessary to allow God's solution, your soul's solution, the *perfect solution* to your problem to manifest itself.

You have to be a magician who produces *Light*, not one who produces what he or she thinks the audience wants to see. You do not want the same old card trick, you do not want the same old production of doves, you do not want the same old levitation trick. You need something that *works*, something that is *pure* magic; something that changes your life, Blessed Reader.

Try this meditation in conjunction with what my friend *Silver Star* has said about silence (*Michael:* a further reference to a lecture by *Silver Star* featured on our website), and if you do this you will build up Light that can be used by your soul so that you can see clearly.

Magic is simply seeing clearly.

Spiritual magic is not the production of illusions. Spiritual magic is the production of truth through Light that penetrates, that breaks away, that tears down the illusion – whether that illusion be an illusion of illness, of poverty, of loneliness, of insecurity, of perversion… whatever you wish to change you *can* change by using this meditation.

And you will say: 'Well, Joseph, this has nothing to do with churches and stained glass and statues and pews and dogma.'

No, *thank God!*

I kneel down and clasp my hands together and say: *Thank God it does not* – for those things of ritual and religion also restrict you. This meditation is a contemporary one designed to free you from those things and to surround you with Light so that you can help yourself and God can help you from within. If you want stained glass solutions do not come to me. If you want dogma do not come to me. I want nothing to do with such handcuffs! I am interested in liberating your mind, in liberating your life and in liberating this world.

(*Michael:* to conclude *Joseph* addresses our little and, by this stage, very soggy group…)

Thank you for this extra opportunity to add an interesting footnote or an extra small chapter to my second book and I look forward to meeting you at the appointed time for the usual continuation of our discussions in order to produce the second book in the series.

May God bless you and keep you and guide you my precious children.

Chapter 9

Questioning your approach to religion

Michael's notes. *Joseph* never wraps something up when he feels it needs to be said outright. He always speaks as though he is holding a metaphorical stopwatch in one hand and there is only a certain amount of time left for us to address our problems and to change things here for the better. The following chapter on religion was delivered in his usual dynamic, passionate style, and pulls no punches in getting straight to the point. It will prove, without a doubt, to be shocking stuff for some readers, whilst for others it will confirm and reinforce something they already believe. If you belong to the former group I would please, and with the greatest of respect and Love, ask you to quietly read the chapter again, and perhaps for a third time, until you recognise the Love that shines from every word, the concern that *Joseph* has for you, for all mankind, and for the Earth, and his urgent need, because of the limited amount of time we have left in which to get things right, to make us recognise and to shake us free from some of our entrenched ideas.

Joseph speaks. The chapter this morning is going to cause quite a stir amongst your readers because it is a subject that people do not face up to, do not think about and, as a result of this, wars are waged, there is violence and prejudice and a harmful 'non-thinking'.

The subject is *religion* and I am going to make some enemies here, I am sure, but also make some friends I hope, because what I am about to say will resonate with certain people reading this book.

God is not religion.

Religion is nothing to do with God.

Heresy!

Blasphemy!

...and yet the truth! The world exists *despite* religion. You exist *despite* religion. Your association with God exists *despite* religion.

...Why do you *need* religion?

'There are many ways to God,' say those who are religious and again they say, 'There is a grain of truth in every religion – there is a thread that leads to God.' Yes, there is, because one man sitting by himself is in communication with God, so when you have many people in a church you are in communication with God... but it is nothing to do with the *doctrine* of that church.

God has put laws into the universe but those laws are not written down so that you can read them and say: 'I must do this and I must not do that.' The laws are consequences and effects so that, as you progress through life, if you act in a certain way there are consequences and if you act in another way there are effects: effects on yourself, on your own soul and on the souls of the people that you touch. So God is not lecturing you, God is not saying: 'Do this. Do that.' God is saying: 'My child, learn!' The difference in many of your religions is that they say: 'Do this! Don't do that! This is what you must believe or you are excluded from Heaven, you are excluded from salvation, you are excluded from spiritual-progress.'

...Nonsense!

Nonsense!

Each soul is progressing.

Each soul is progressing by working within the laws that God has built into the physical universe and the spiritual universe and built into *you* because you are a fragment of God. So, built within yourself is something that you refer to as 'conscience'. And conscience is a guiding light saying to you: 'Maybe this path is not the one to travel.' Or: 'Maybe this path is the one that you should go down.' And because the laws are built within you, you can *go within* for all the instruction you need as to how to approach your God and how to approach each other.

There is no religion – it is a man-made construct.

The reason I am telling you this today is not to deconstruct your ideas on religion, is not to strip away everything that you hold true, but to say that *religion causes so much evil on your world.*

Religion causes war; religion causes prejudice against certain areas of mankind and certain areas of society. *Religion is one of the greatest evils* and in the future for your world you will have to amalgamate. You will have your different approaches to God, yes, but you cannot allow dogma to keep you apart. You cannot wage war in the name of religion; you cannot kill someone in the name of religion. Where is the logic in that?

Your religions need to be filled with Love and they are not. If you watch a minister or a priest at work and they are filled with Love, then it doesn't matter what they are saying; you will feel a warmth towards and from that person. But when you see ministers and priests simply spouting words and there is a coldness about them, then you should move away from the instructions you are being given by those people because they do not come from God.

The true 'religion' is Love.

If you could condense everything that God wants you to do into one word – that one word would be *Love*.

Rip up your Bible! What heresy! *Rip up your Bible!* Once the words have gone into your soul rip them up! Otherwise you are referring constantly to the written word and the written word is cold, the written word is dead – it has no Love in it. The advanced souls who tried to teach you tried to pass on the simple message that God is Love, that you are Love and that, if you put Love into every aspect of your being, every aspect of your life, then the world goes according to God's plan. Man has a tendency to want to organise, to write down, to solidify, to crystallise and *you cannot do that with the word of God*, you cannot do that with the word of advanced souls.

A time is coming when many religions will be overthrown – not by violence but by people withdrawing from them and saying, 'This contains nothing for me; this is a vacuum.' But there has to be something to *replace* that approach to God. It is the approach to God that is wrong and the approach to each other and to yourselves that is wrong. You have to replace religion with what has always been the basis of God's relationship with man and man's relationship with his fellow man... and that is Love.

Love is misinterpreted; Love is misused around your planet. You are shown ideals of Love, you are shown romantic views of love, you are shown soft views of love. But we are not 'soft'. We bring Love to you but is a Love that is able to be used; it is a Love that exists in the dark places around the world; it is a Love that seeks to uphold and maintain those poor souls that have nothing in their lives. This is the Love you should have for others; not a love that considers self but a Love that is *in action* in everything that you do. If you make a drink for someone you should put Love into it. If you listen to someone, listen to what they are saying with Love, no matter how tedious their words may seem to you. If you have to discipline someone to return them to the path of Love then do it with Love; do not do it with anger. Love does not mean that you sit in a circle twenty-four hours a day and hug each other and accomplish nothing! Love is the spirit of God *in action* going from one soul to another and *it is Love that this world needs.*

To change this world you first of all have to look at your religions and you have to ask: 'Do they contain Love? In what I am being told to do is there Love? In approaching other people through the confines of my religion, am I loving them?' And you have some hard tasks ahead of you because, if you have a gnawing feeling within you that your religion is not satisfying you then you owe it to yourself and to your God and to the future of your planet to examine that feeling, to see where it takes you, to be confident enough to open up those questions in your mind and say, 'Is this religion right for me? Does it serve me? Does it serve my community? Does it serve the brothers and sisters I sit in church with?' And if the answer is 'no', do not feel guilty because that answer comes from Love, comes from the God within you.

And having examined your religion, if you find it wanting, you then have to be brave enough to *reject* it. At this point, many people will say: 'Oh, no! If I reject my religion, I reject God.'

No.

The two are separate; you have to separate your religious beliefs, your religious doctrines, from your view of God. Religion separates you from God far more than if you had no religion and were sitting by yourself on an island and were communicating with your God from within.

So, you have to examine your religion first and if it comes up short, you have to have the courage to reject it. And then, *Joseph*, what do I do? Then you sit quietly and you say: 'God, I have been controlled for many years; I have been blindfolded for many years. I wish to help the Earth, I wish to help myself. I wish to help my fellow beings …What do you want me to do?'…And a voice will come from within that will motivate you. Do not expect God to speak to you in a thunderous voice from outside yourself. He will give you *intentions*; He will give you *inspirations* as to what you should do next. And once you have freed yourself from the shackles, from the confines of doctrines that have no place in the name of Love in God's universe, then you will attract towards yourself the souls and the situations that you need in order to progress, to get closer to your God and to do the work that you are supposed to do.

We often weep when we see religious meetings; we weep because we see souls that are controlled purely through the mind – through the physical mind. We see manipulation, we see ego, we see all the things that you say are the worst aspects of your society in operation from those souls who are supposed to be leading you religiously. We see squabbles amongst religious representatives and one doctrine put up against another doctrine to say: 'Mine is the best.' 'No, *mine* is the best!' 'No, *this* is what the people should believe.' And the people are in *shackles* because the people are not listening to the God within. They are not *able* to listen to the God within because they are imprisoned within their minds by what they are told to believe.

How can you harm a hair of someone else's head in the name of religion?

Are you saying that that is what your God wishes you to do? Are you saying that your God has given to you exclusively the pathway to Heaven and that everyone else is out of the picture because they do not believe what you believe? Think with your heart! Begin to question and deconstruct some of your beliefs that come up short. Do you, for example, believe that your God is a punishing God; that your God wants you to go from this place, which is hell on Earth (and mankind has created it), to an even greater hell because you do not think in a certain way, because you do not act in a certain way, because you do not toe the line, because you are in peril and in sin?

Nonsense!

Your God is a God of Love. Your God at no stage in your infinite existence *ever judges you* but always supports you. You judge yourself. You decide the path that you take back to the Godhead. Your God does not advocate violence as a means to spreading His word. How can He? Would it not be similar to one body attacking itself? Would it not be similar to taking a knife and plunging it into yourself and saying: 'This is what I want you to do in my name – I want you to damage part of me!' If you damage another soul you damage part of God. If you take another's life, you damage part of God. If all souls are equal children of God – *and they are* – how can you do this? How can you justify this in the name of religion?

How?

How?!

Time to think! To question. ...How can you do this?

You have churches that are half empty and you have churches full of *empty people* because their lives are not touched by Love. The Love is restricted: 'I cannot think this way; I cannot act that way. God doesn't want me to do this. God doesn't want me to do that.'

The task of brothers and sisters who are acting in Love is, within the next few decades, to sweep away the remnants of those religions that no longer have a place on Earth and to educate those people by sending Love to them.

And that is a great task, because many souls prefer the 'corridor' that they have to walk along mentally to the expanse and the scenery outside of that corridor because it is safe, it is easy, they don't need to think from the heart. But *you* do. If you are reading this book and these words resonate with you, then in order to be a worker for the Light, a worker for Love, a worker for God, you have to divest yourself of doctrines that are no longer of use to you. You have to then send out Love into the world on a daily basis.

You, as a soul within the illusion, are beginning to *ask things of yourself*, which is why you are reading this book. Globally souls are beginning to ask things of themselves and say, 'There must be another way. Things are not changing. There must be another way. Where have we got it wrong? How do we get it right?' Well, one area where you have got it wrong is in the area of religion.

I must emphasise here that I am not saying that every religious representative is misled and that no religious representative is loving. Quite the opposite! There are wonderful, loving people within the confines of religion but you will find that the loving people within the confines of religion have somehow overcome some of those confines and are not quite linked to the centre of that religion as the other representatives are. If they were they would be restricted in their ability to Love and to help people.

Each one of you is a minister. Think about the term 'minister' – someone who can minister to others. You can minister anything to others: you can give them help, you can send them your anger, your violence or your Love … and you are asked to send Love to the world.

We come to talk to you to try and sweep away the barriers that you have placed around yourself and one of the purposes of this book is to remove barriers.

I worshipped different gods in different incarnations and for me, as I look back through the record of my existence on Earth, I can see that those times when I mistakenly worshipped various deities and various doctrines were karmic opportunities because, in seeing what I shouldn't worship, I finally found what I *should* worship: freedom, Love and the God within.

I said that this chapter would be controversial and it is. Do not misunderstand me, I do not wish to take a torch to the world's religions – I bring instead a torch of Light... Yes! To say to those who are steeped in so much doctrine that they cannot think, 'Here is the Light. Let the Light shine on the words of your religion, let it shine into your Bibles, let it illuminate the words, let it shine in your minds so that you have enough strength, enough will power to examine what is being said to you. Do not accept blindly.'

You have the figure on Earth of 'blind justice' that you use in your courts and place outside your courthouses. Are you suffering from blind justice? Take off the blindfold. Your God will not smite you down; your God will not destroy you for thinking from the heart, for using your mind, for using your faculties to examine what you have been told.

If you examine what you have been told and it makes perfect sense to you and you do not wish to change, then you are blessed. Continue along that path. But if there are chinks in the armour of your religion then it is time perhaps to look at something else, at a simpler way. Does your religion, for example, help people or does it sit on a platform and say: 'How holy we are, how poor you are?'

What have you done today – today as you are reading this chapter – to help people? Did you begin your day by sending Love into the world? Did you begin your day by loving yourself? Did you begin your day via a conversation with your God? Do you *ever* do these things? If you pray for people, do you pray for them to be altered according to

God's will *according to your religion*? That is no prayer! That goes nowhere; that has no energy. Your prayers should be that the Love of God within people is manifest. In praying this way you heal them, in praying this way you begin their own journey into knowledge – true spiritual knowledge. If you *dictate* in your prayers then they are not prayers. If your prayer is that people who are not of your religion should be of your religion, that is not a prayer and it is not right; you do not have the right to choose for other people.

Love is the only way to bring to people around to the fact from their hearts that they are God. Love is the only way to change people from their violent ways, to get them to put aside their violent ways, to make them see. *Your task is to make people see.* They are blinded: blinded by words, blinded by organisations, blinded by aspects of this illusion that have no place in the future of this world...

... if there *is* to be a future for this world.

Tell me, Reader, *which* is the one, true religion? Which of the many religions around your world is the true religion? Which is God's religion? And if you say: 'It is mine,' then does everyone else have no path back to God? Is there a way into your religion? Will you all be saved? Do you need to be saved? Well, yes, you do – you need to be saved from yourselves, from your minds that are so plugged into this way of thinking and not *feeling* that you cannot identify how you should be acting whilst you are on this Earth.

When I was a boy in Atlantis I got up very early one morning and there were three hills – beautiful, *beautiful* hills – and I sat on a hill opposite them and looked over at them at dawn and I found my God because I became *one* with those hills, and with the dawn, and with the air, and with the sounds of the world and I found my God. No religion necessary! *No religion necessary* – simply a communion with God. And in subsequent lives I did belong to certain religious causes but then I had incarnated at a time when the effects of The Fall of mankind were being felt around this world but I had the sense eventually to say, 'This is not for me.'

I seem to have been very harsh this morning... or perhaps very forthright, but I *have* to be. If you do not show the child another way then the child will always be on the path it is on. If the child does not have access to that other way from within, how can it change?

We are worried, concerned, upset by the things that are said in the name of God. Many religions say, 'You should not blaspheme, you should not take God's name in vain,' and yet *the whole set up of such religions is a blasphemy*. That is taking the name of God in vain; that is what it means – not to swear, not to call God a name – but to believe in things that in reality are blasphemy against God's Love. So many religions take, throughout their existence, the name of God in vain because the name of God is *Love. The name of God is Love!* Not any complex, mystical name for God – there is only one word for God and it is 'Love'.

I do not seek forgiveness in shaking you up. This book is intended to shake you up. This book is intended to change you – not because of my words but because of my *hope* that, in reading these words, you will go within, you will question. One of the greatest gifts you have been given is the ability to question and to discern for yourself. In many religions you do not use that ability; you prefer instead to be led, to be told: 'This is how it is. These are the barriers, these are the borders. You act in this way and do not overstep the barrier on either side of you.' Be brave! In connecting with God *be brave*. In changing this world *be brave*. And in order to change this world you have to be brave enough to ask questions.

If this book disturbs you, that is wonderful. If you are disturbed by aspects of your religion, that is wonderful. Do not put a lid on your disturbance or on your unease but examine it. Your disturbance comes from the God within saying: 'No! No! **No!** There is another way!'

Are you in shackles or are you truly free? If you are part of a doctrine that excludes others, part of a doctrine that proclaims violence as the way, part of a doctrine that seeks only to glorify *itself* – then you are in shackles, you are in chains, you are in prison.

Begin to think from the heart, begin to question those things that disturb you. That disturbance is there for a reason; you are not being blasphemous by examining the disturbance. You are not being untrue to God's doctrine by examining the disturbance but you are being untrue to yourself by *ignoring* it.

We look forward to a time when each person on Earth communicates personally and in groups with the God within, where each person links to every other person without a label, without a barrier, without the fear that causes you to want to convert everyone who is not of you into what you are; a time when you celebrate your diversity and realise your Oneness at the same time: 'I am different than you are as an individual; I am identical to you as part of God.'

I spoke about Light as a weapon recently and I would like to end this chapter by talking briefly about Love. Love and Light are the same thing but what is Love?

What is Love?

At the core of its meaning, what is that word about? It is about recognition – recognition of who you are, recognition of who the other is, recognition that there is in reality no 'other' – only yourself, only God reflected in hundreds and thousands and millions of people.

Love is also harmony. Harmony: a Oneness of vibration, a vibration of peace that you find when you accept the other person for what they are, when you accept yourself for what you are, when you seek not to control or to violate the other person's personality. Harmony: when you learn to vibrate for a time each day on a God-level to receive

110

information, to receive instruction that is not based on discipline but is based on Love, is based on your God transmitting a harmonious plan for the evolution of your soul through to your heart and to the hearts of others.

Love is action. Love does not judge. Love is helping, Love is supporting, Love is tolerating, Love is giving – because all these things lead back to harmony. Love is investing your time in others because you appreciate that others are part of you.

Love is investing time now in the Earth so that the generations to come will be lifted out of the darkness that they placed themselves in long ago.

Love is Oneness. Love is *all* – a concept that can only truly be felt and can never adequately be expressed in the written word. Love is a knowing from within.

God is Love. Love is God. The two are interchangeable because they are the same thing.

Chapter 10

Freeing yourself from oppressive tendencies

Michael's notes. This is the first of two chapters given to us on the same morning (Chapter 11 followed straight on from this communication after the shortest of breaks). *Joseph* had advised that we 'double up' our session as he felt conditions would be a little difficult around the end of the year with regard to bringing through information effectively. Shortly before Christmas arrived what he meant became apparent – a week before the holiday my mother fell and broke her hip and spent a month in hospital. Hospital visiting, preparation for her return to her home and other related preoccupations ruled out any communication with *Joseph* during that four week period.

Joseph speaks. What I would like to talk about first of all today is oppression, its prevalence in society and the problems it causes. Every human being strives to get what they want from life: be it a material satisfaction, a romantic satisfaction, a spiritual satisfaction. Most people's lives are concerned with obtaining what they want from life *all the time*. Every human being wants what *they* want and their world-view, that is their individual perception of physical 'reality' coloured by their wishes and desires is, they believe, the correct one.

So, how do human beings attempt to manifest what they desire around themselves? There are several ways to get what you want but, invariably, many people on Earth choose *oppression* as a means of trying to manifest their personal world-view. By oppression I mean that, in order to get what they want, very often they will try to mould other souls to their will.

Oppression begins in the playground with the bully – the person who uses more aggression than the others – attempting to dominate the other children so that he or she gets what they want.

In work situations too people often oppress each other to get what they want. Employers, for example, feel that if they rule through strictness, through terror, through frightening people, their workers will give them exactly what they want, and employees attempt to dominate other employees in order to award themselves a higher personal status.

In many personal relationships one partner will dominate the other and seek, through oppression, to mould that relationship into the world-view that they have of it and manifest what they want from it.

On a national scale, the linked concept of politics or the linked concept of religion (by 'linked concepts' I mean the shared desires of a number of souls united in trying to obtain what they want) often seeks to oppress anything that is not of that concept and to bend it to its will. In the past you have had 'holy' crusades and 'holy' wars where, in the name of religion, souls have sought to oppress others and to bend them to their world–view with the intention of shaping them into a physical manifestation of what those souls want from life.

Also, to a large extent many people regard others as 'friends' or 'enemies' dependent on what they can give them according to their world-view of what they desire.

So, your society is built to a large extent upon oppression, upon aggressive souls subduing less aggressive souls, bending those less aggressive souls to their will in the hope that when they wake each morning having oppressed someone, or some nation, or some concept the day before, they will feel they are a little closer on that morning to having obtained what they want from life.

The problem is what they want from life *changes*. Having oppressed a situation, or a person, or a nation and obtained their initial world-view of what they feel they want they quickly find that they are still unfulfilled. When you get what you think you want on a level that is not linked with a high spiritual intent *there is no fulfilment*. You experience only emptiness as your 'triumph' does not measure up to how you thought you would feel in the circumstances following you getting what you felt you wanted in life. You therefore change your view of what you desire constantly in an attempt to find fulfilment, and you resent the people and situations you have oppressed previously because, in your world-view, it is their fault for not having brought you what you desired.

How could they?

If you had truly succeeded through the use of oppression and others had given in to your will and you had gained exactly what you wanted you should feel bliss, shouldn't you? You should feel joy, shouldn't you? In controlling people and situations successfully you would have moulded the world into exactly what you wanted it to be. The truth is no soul who has ever oppressed anyone else has ever found satisfaction from having done so. Oppression doesn't work! Oppression results only in spiritual emptiness. It is a mistake. It is a transgression against others and against yourself.

You cannot get what you want ever, ever, **ever** by using oppression.

I have to take this back to its root and make you understand that what you as a 'physical being' think you want and what you as a soul *actually* want are two *extremely different* things.

The soul at its core craves harmony, craves reunification with God. That need – and it is a need that can only be fulfilled by reunification in mind and in intent with God – is at the core of all that is wrong in the world. You feel that you need to change people and objects and situations in order to feel fulfilled, when in fact you need to change *yourself*, to change your perception. And this can be done in an instant by realising that your only need is for the God within and for a reunification with that Love you separated yourself from millennia ago through *your own transgression of thought.*

Many, many, *many* years ago, you decided – souls on Earth decided – that they would take a different path, that they knew better than God as to how the physical universe should evolve and, as a result of that, there was a 'separation'. Not a separation sanctioned or brought about by God but a separation as a result of your vibrationary rate changing to *include* the reality (in fact, an illusion) that you wanted around you at that time and to *exclude* the voice of God. You thought you knew better than God. You refused to listen to God, and so you changed your vibrationary rate to exclude the voice of God. The voice of God is still within you but you cannot normally hear it because you are tuned into a different vibration.

The time has come to realise that you are still a part of God; that God did not throw you out – you threw yourselves out – and to sit and to consider, from a spiritual angle, what you *really* want. And what you *really* want is to reconnect with God; what you *really* want is to re-experience the bliss of God's Love flowing through you. The irony is that it flows through you at every minute, at every second, and it is yours *now*. You cry out to God and say, 'God, I am not happy. God, I need this. I want that. Why are other people not like me?' And, even worse, sometimes in God's name you say, 'I will oppress situations and people to make them more like I and You want them to be, Father. Together, You and I want them to be a certain way.'

No.

No!

No!

First rediscover God and then you will stop oppressing people, you will stop fighting with people, you will stop controlling people so that they, in your view, can make you happy by doing what you want them to do. You will never find fulfilment in that way. You will never find fulfilment by controlling your wife, your husband, your children, your animals, your work-mates, your political groups, your religious groups, other countries, other cultures. You cannot ever make yourself happy by doing this, by oppressing others. That is not to say that other souls and yourself do not make mistakes, that there is not a more fulfilling way to live, that there is not a better world-view for all that is worth creating, but you do not create that world-view, you do not make it a reality, you do not bring to light and transform people's mistakes by oppressing them. You do it by *changing yourself first*, by reverting to what you are and by listening to the God within and then by emanating that God-Light out into the world around you.

A preparation for Meditation.

As a preparation for this liberating meditation sit quietly, enveloping yourself in God's Light for a few minutes and consider first, before you approach God, the ways in which you might be oppressing people and yourself.

Begin with yourself. Do you try to control – to oppress - *yourself*? Are you putting limits on what you can do? Are you oppressing yourself, being violent with yourself within your own psyche (a great many people do this to themselves) and do you kick yourself, metaphorically, because you want to 'be' in a certain way and find that you are not? Do you expect too much of yourself and berate yourself when you do not succeed and do not live up to your own expectations? If the answer is 'yes' then you are oppressing *yourself* and, for the time of this meditation, for the time of this quietness, let go of that self oppression; accept and love yourself as you are at this moment.

Next consider those closest to you – your partners, your parents – how do you react to them? Do you oppress them? Do you use them in certain ways to get what you want? Do you bend them to make them conform to your view of how they should act towards you? Be honest with yourself at this point and let go of any need on a physical level, on a mental level, on an emotional level, to control your partners and your parents.

Look at how you treat your friends. Are they truly your friends or do you only ring them, only contact them, when you want them to do something for you? Are they only your friends when they do what you want them to do and when they don't are they not your friends? Is this how friendship should be? Let go of any need to oppress and to control your friends.

Next consider your employer or your employees. Are you oppressing the people at work? Are you manipulating your employer or employees through oppression to get what you want out of your work situation?

In all these situations – with your friends, with your parents, with your partners, with your employers – if you were *to give* rather than *to oppress* you would receive Love and harmony in return. If you were to set people free to do what they wanted to do they would never leave you. If you were to be considerate in your dealings with others (and try to understand that they, too, are mistakenly attempting to manifest a personal world-view that requires that they try to control and oppress others) then you would look at their motives differently and be able to forgive more.

But, to return to your meditation, you need to let go of your control and your oppression of others in intimate family groups, in friendship groups, in work and globally at this point.

The Meditation.

Now... become very still and see – in the darkness around you as you sit with eyes closed, free from the noise and the clutter of human life, of human society – see a light in front of you: a little pin-point of light. See that light expand. See it as a silver light that moves towards you, enters your solar plexus and, as it does so, spreads out to envelop you, to cleanse you, to take away your need to control your world and the worlds of others.

Then see in front of you a gold light: a light that contains such Love for you that you feel you will melt; a light that is the Light of God. See that Light moving towards you and entering your solar plexus. See it changing the silver light that is enveloping you into a gold light. Feel the warmth from that Light. Realise that that Light is your connection to God, that that Light *is* God and that *you and the Light are the same thing*. And then hear, listen, *feel* the intent of that Light. That Light has only one intent – to love you – nothing more. That Light requires nothing from you except that you acknowledge it for your own greater good.

Consider this as you sit within that Light for a few minutes... the Light is not trying to control you. It does not require you to be of a certain religion, of a certain colour, of a certain financial status, of a certain political view, of a certain level of intelligence, of a certain sexual persuasion. That Light simply requires you *to be* within it and to share the peace that that Light brings to you with others.

This is where you began – within the Light. This is where you were born as a soul. This is where you were created absolutely free – not to condemn, not to oppress, but to nurture, to love, to harmonise with all Creation.

Listen at this point in your meditation to what the Light says to you – either through direct speech or through your senses, through your intuition, through a feeling that comes over you, and know that God requires nothing from you except that you *be*; know that *you are Him and He is you*.

Holding yourself in the Light forgive yourself for all the times that you have sought to control others. And if you want to change others (and your only intention in wanting to change others should be to make them aware of the Light as you are perceiving it at this moment) send it out to them, see them enveloped in the same Light whilst you are in your meditation and do not oppress, do not say, 'You can only have this Light if you conform to my world-view.' The Light is theirs – as it is yours – by spiritual birthright.

Spread this Light to all world situations. Never condemn. In condemning you separate yourself from the Light and your prayer has no power. It is only in sending out the Light, in being a giver of Light without condition, without judgement, without prerequisites, that you allow that Light to do its job ...and that job is to re-unify all other souls into the Light.

(*Michael:* me again – and you know what I'm going to say: as you end this meditation remember to ask God to protect you and to guide you and to close your chakras for you. Sorry – but it's *important*.)

From the moment you read this and attempt to meditate in this way, I would ask you to consider living your life in a different way – not from a core of oppression (which is born out of fear) but from a core of total commitment to the God within. This is a non-religious thing to do – you are simply saying: 'I have found you, Father, and I wish others to find you, Father, so I send the Light out to them.' Begin to live your life without oppressing others and see how life blossoms around you.

Through oppression you seek to hold on to friendships, relationships, political views, religious views, and you do all this out of fear. When you give the Light out there is no need to fear. People will recognise in you the fact that you have found your foundation, your core; the fact that you are harmonious; the fact that you mean them no harm; the fact that **you do not want** – and they will flock to you. You will never be lonely, your health will improve (because many of the aliments you suffer from are due to an imbalance within your soul that is brought about by your seeking to control life in a particular way), your thoughts will be more productive, more creative, and you will truly be making a difference in that you will be reuniting souls with their spiritual birthright through sending the Light out to them unconditionally.

When you connect to your God in this way and know, from within yourself, that you are part of everything, it is your *birthday*, because you are remembering that point at which you were individualised from the Light, that point at which you were made a personal viewpoint from the *Whole* and which you have forgotten until now. *Happy Birthday!*

My intention with the books in this series is to make you aware of who you are, make you aware of where you have gone wrong, make you aware of how to put things right and make you aware of where you are going to next, but I do not do any of this by oppressing you, by bending you to my viewpoint. My viewpoints are given freely and in Love. You can reject them if you wish ...but before you do so ask yourself, 'Am I truly happy? Do I know where I am going? Am I afraid of death? Am I afraid of losing the love of others? Am I afraid of losing my health? Am I afraid each day of living that day? Am I afraid within my religious beliefs or within my political beliefs? Do I find fulfilment in my life? Am I truly in control as I want to be or do I simply try to control others to make sense of a world that I do not understand?'

Once you connect with the God within everything else makes sense and you stop fighting and start listening, you extend your lifespan, you extend your capabilities because God-Light flows through you and you become a beacon for peace.

The task ahead of you is both simple and difficult. It is simple in that all you have to do is connect with the God-Light within you and send it out. It is difficult because many people will not understand what you are trying to do. ...So do not tell them! Work secretly; work silently. You have to build up in them a spiritual 'charge' over days and weeks and months and years. You have to build up in them enough Light that they (as the spiritual beings they really are) can see past the illusions, the constructs they have put around themselves, and begin to reach within for answers.

You will not change the murderer today; you will not change the war machine today ...but you *will change the murderer and the war machine tomorrow* by the work you put in today, which contributes towards that point where souls will have an epiphany, where they will realise who they are. God works slowly but if you are building a building you do not place it on quicksand – you make sure the foundations are right and rock steady and then the building stands forever.

Send out Love but do not expect to be rewarded, do not expect to see an instant change in people (although there *will* be with certain souls who will only need that little extra guidance to discover again who they are; to remember who they are, and the change in them will be a rapid one) but see yourself as cleansing the souls you send Light to, building up enough illumination for them to be able to see out of the darkness they have placed themselves in. And try very hard not to oppress people. You have the free will to do so as you have the free will to do anything, but it is not the right thing to do. God does not control. God does not rule. God simply wants you to be the expression of Him that you were individualised in order to be.

(Michael: Joseph breaks communication at this stage.)

Joseph. This is the break point of the communication and we will continue with another theme after a suitable period of rest.

Chapter 11

Finding your peace within

Joseph speaks. The subject of today's second talk is peace.

Peace is something that all nations aspire to – *at least in words* – and it is something that individuals also aspire to:

'I wish I could have peace in my life.'

'If only I had a little peace I would feel better.'

'Why can't we live in peace?'

'Why can't there be peace on Earth?'

There is no peace on Earth because you do not understand the concept of peace.

Peace is a continuous state and not something that is simply a resolution to your current problems; peace is a knowledge of God; a state of harmonious vibration.

The reason you cannot find peace is because you wish there to be *conditional peace.* You wish there to be a certain outcome of a war, for example, so that certain political views, certain power structures, are upheld. I am now going to say something to you which will be controversial at very least: in all of your wars, at the end of each of your wars, there has never truly been peace. There has been a cessation of hostilities but no peace because, if there had truly been peace there would be no further wars.

Peace is an unconditional state of rest. It is a state of rest of aggression, if you like, a state of rest of hostilities, a state of rest of domination, a state of rest of control of others. It is a relinquishing of all of these things. And peace has a vibrational value – *peace exists as a state of non-aggressive attraction between spiritual beings.*

I had better explain that.

Harmony is peace and peace is a state of recognition within souls of *themselves in others – of themselves as God in others.*

Once you recognise yourself in others, how can you destroy others? How can you control others? How can you seek to impose your views on others against their will? At the point at which you connect with God there is a universal vibration, it is a vibration that runs through you and through everything – you are part of the universal sea of consciousness. The state of peace is experienced when you operate from that core of Oneness from God and extend yourself outwards into your daily lives from that Oneness with God. Peace cannot really occur on material and physical levels, at least not until you re-recognise your dependence on God. (*I am sorry I am having more difficulty in putting forth my views than I had earlier with you* [Michael: Joseph is referring to the first communication given earlier this same morning] *and the reason for this is because I am attempting to describe spiritual concepts in physical terms.*)

Peace is a state of *knowing*, peace is a state of *being* and, if you could see the vibrations of peace, you would see a light – rather like a sea of light – that is not buffeted but is calm; a sea that is unaffected by

124

storms or tides and is still like a millpond – a quiet sea of light. That is the condition of peace and that condition, that vibration, is a nourishing vibration. When souls tune into it, tap into it, it feeds them. It is a vibration that does no harm, it is a vibration that reacts with the vibrations of the individual soul and brings a state of wellbeing to them. It nourishes the molecules of the spirit it connects with. It also brings a level of harmony to the mental state of that spirit. The vibration of peace is not static but calm, without turmoil, without eddies, swirls and tides.

When a spirit is incarnated into the flesh the effects of The Field on that spirit create, within that spirit's perception, discord. A spirit being born today, for example, is being born into The Field of consciousness that has existed for millions of years and the state of The Field at the moment is (as I have said previously) set to negativity, set to violence and aggression. When the soul is incarnated into The Field *initially* it is at peace; the vibration within it is that calm vibration from God, that harmony that brings with it health and wellbeing and intuition and a sense of purpose. Immediately the child is born into this world it is set upon, as it were, by discordant vibrations. Consider what happens to a baby as it is brought into this world. It is brought into this world by a shock, by a slap. Its first experience of this place is of pain and of breathing in a lung full of air and of crying. Infants are not brought into this world in a happy state; they are introduced to this level of illusion through violence. And there is sown within them, as they sleep peacefully after having been brought into this world by violence, a growing discord which changes the vibration of peace which is their natural state.

Then, as they grow older and more experienced on this level, they are beset by other problems. They are beset by those who would (as I said previously) oppress them. They find that the world is divided into factions: religious factions, political factions; they discover that there are souls who will exert violence in order to get what they want, that there are perversions of the soul that cause souls to act in a very base way. And all these aspects of life on Earth within the illusion of The Field gradually mask and change the vibration of peace which is the rest-state of the soul.

Each soul on Earth knows within itself at God–level that it requires peace, that it requires to get back to that state of bliss, that state of total non-worry, that state of total calm that it initially brings with it to the Earth plane – and so it struggles to look for and to manifest that state of vibration on a physical level. We are back to: 'I want peace.' 'I need peace.' 'We need peace on Earth.' 'This war should end in peace.' but your peace on Earth (whether it is personal or global or national) is *conditional*. It is peace 'as long as you behave in the way I want you to behave'; it is peace 'as long as I am in certain conditions, have certain securities, have certain affections.' So your concept of peace is always conditional, it is 'as long as the right side wins', it is 'as long as someone shuts up and doesn't cause me any more problems.' It is always conditional, yet peace on a God-level is a state that does not have conditions attached to it – its only 'condition' is that you tune into it, as with other things spiritual.

Peace will never be found on Earth until you find the peace within.

In finding the peace within, in re-resonating with that birth-vibration, you cannot be at odds with anyone because, when you link into that peace-vibration, you discover that everyone else has it within themselves; that you are, in fact, fighting yourself if you want a certain outcome in a war, that you are fighting yourself if you want a certain outcome within a family unit. You have to get back to recognising the peace within.

In this book I talk a lot about meditation, about becoming quiet, becoming peaceful, because this is the only way to change things on your level of consciousness. Only by seeking all the answers *inside* can you project them *outside* and into The Field to generate enough Light into The Field to change its inherent vibrations, which at the moment are non-peaceful, which at the moment are self-seeking, which at the moment are designed to, from cradle to grave, promote unrest within the individual and within the group consciousness on Earth so that all souls are dependent on The Field. The Field seeks the attention of individuals and the group consciousness to maintain itself. The Field has developed an ego and that ego is a negative vibration. And so you are slaves to The Field whilst you are in it, excepting those souls who have found peace and God within themselves... and those souls feel displaced because they know that their natural state is not the state of The Field they have been born into.

The only way to discover peace, to create peace on Earth, is not to *create* it in yourself (because it already exists within yourself) but to *rediscover* it within yourself, and the key to finding peace within yourself is through *letting go*. In those moments when you sit quietly you will find that you bring into your meditations all the cares of your day, all the cares of your life: 'I am worried about my health, I am worried about my finances, I am worried about my family members, I am worried about my house, I am worried about so many things' ...and all these worries are projected onto you by The Field so that you maintain The Field in its current state. This, I hope, explains why, when someone is working spiritually, it seems such a difficult task, because The Field reacts against that which is different, that which is alien to it, that which threatens its existence in its current form. So immediately you sit (until you are trained... until you have trained yourself) you will find that you have distractions, that you have worries.

If you are ever to reach the field of peace that is within you and to project that peace outwards into the greater field – the physical *illusion* – you have to get rid of the worries of the day, you have to let them go. There are many ways of doing this but perhaps the easiest is to leave them, in your imagination, outside the 'door to your meditation chamber'. As you enter into your meditation, say to yourself: 'Well, I am leaving all my worries outside of myself. I am hanging them on a peg by the door, and if I choose to take them up again when I come out of my mediation I will do so. ... But maybe I won't.' (Hopefully, you won't.) Leave them 'in a bag by the door' so that, as you become quiet, you are not pulling into your meditation the worries that cause you so many distractions on a physical and mental level. Then, when you have left your worries 'by the door', you are in a fit state to seek peace.

It matters not what you visualise: you may see yourself under a moon in a wood, or on a seashore, or nowhere at all – perhaps just floating in Light. Within that visual concept you build in your meditation you now have to seek the peace of God, and the easiest way to connect with the peace of God is, having let go of your worries (having left them 'by the door' as you came into your meditation chamber of the imagination) to also *let go of yourself*. What a difficult thing to do! And how you will *fear* letting go of yourself: 'What can *Joseph* mean, 'letting go' of myself? If I let go of myself, will I die? Will I ever find myself again? Will I be able to claw my way out of my meditation back into the physical field that I loathe so much and love so much at the same time?'

I am talking about letting go of the complex shell of thoughts that you surround yourselves with every day of your lives and that you think constitutes you: the 'you' that worries about finances, the 'you' that has biases towards people and organisations, the 'you' that perhaps suffers from certain physical ailments, day after day. All those things are *of* you but are not *you*. They are of the physical self but not of the spirit self. Your spirit self knows nothing about illness, knows nothing about the mortgage payments, knows nothing about the need to put fuel in the car, knows nothing about a conflict of egos with people around you. So by 'letting go of yourself' I mean letting go of your physical self, letting go of that shell, letting go of all those things that define who you are on a physical level but not on a spiritual level. Letting them float away from you, freeing yourself of them, becoming who you already are: *the unbiased, unchanging Light of God made individual in illusion only in order that you might grow as a soul and bring more information back to God when you return to Him.*

Once you let go of the self you will find yourself – your spirit self – immersed in a wonderful feeling of bliss and contentment, in a timelessness, in a sea of energy … in peace. And you may stay there for a few seconds or minutes or even hours and you will be refreshed and you will know that true peace *can* exist and that peace is an unchanging equation, is a vibration of God, is your natural state, and you will begin to understand why you crave peace so much in all aspects of your life, because it is what you really are and it is what you want to be again.

On a subconscious level you desire peace because it is what you really are.

Now – how do you translate that peace into your world? A difficult equation! A difficult question! Peace exists when you seek to reunite others with you, to reunite others with the God that is within them. So your starting point in your politics, in resolving your conflicts, in finding peace, has got to be: 'What is best for these people on a God-level? What is best for this situation on a God-level? What would God do? What does God require of me in this situation?' When you approach a conflict in this manner, that vibration of peace within you (that is God) is accessible to you and permeates your consciousness with the way of peace pertaining to that particular situation. In other words, you will *know* what to do and you will not have an agenda; you cannot have an agenda when seeking peace.

Peace on Earth between nations is dependent at present on agendas. It is peace but peace with terms attached: 'Peace if you live in the way that I want you to live. Peace if you serve me as I want you to serve me. Peace as long as I get what I want from the equation, from the situation.' True peace can be found only in having the courage to allow the other people involved in the process to rediscover the God within themselves; to allow them their way of life, for example; to allow them their views, even though those views may be alien to you. (And remember to refer to the previous chapter in which I describe how to send Light to people if you are absolutely sure on a God-level that what they are doing is contrary to God's view for this world so that you can, in time, allow them not to be changed by you but to change themselves by having enough of a spiritual charge to seek the God within them for themselves.)

So peace in a way is saying: 'We agree to disagree but we are not going to fall out about it. We agree that we have different views but we understand that those views are simply physical views, they are views that are tied into and contaminated by the illusion. But we have a greater level, you and I, we have a level at which we can agree completely because that level is the peace that runs through you and runs though me and is the vibration that comes from the God within us. At that level we are already at peace, at that level there can be no war between us, no aggression between us, we are already at peace – it is simply a matter of acknowledging it.'

The intention of this book is to give you – individually and collectively – the ammunition with which to flood this illusion with enough Light for it to change. None of the methods I have described to you involve violence, involve oppression of another human being, involve the control of another person's point of view.

It is is a war of peace I am asking you to wage – a war of *peace* – because the problem lies not so much with the other souls within The Field as with The Field itself. The Field itself, which has been given consciousness by millennia of incorrect thinking, has to be reconstructed – deconstructed and reconstructed – it has to find peace, has to be reset to peace, and that will only occur when sufficient Light is poured into The Field that The Field itself becomes a higher vibration and is changed. At the point that The Field itself is changed people will draw on that revised vibration rather than on the anxieties and worries that The Field presents to them currently on a daily basis, and will be fed by The Field rather than being controlled by The Field.

At that point your world changes forever. At that point you rediscover a paradise. At that point there is true peace because you realise that peace has to be worked at, yes, but only has to be worked at in that it is there within you and you have to work to find it.

'*Peace be with you,*' is something that you say in certain of your churches and (because I am a revolutionary) I would ask the ministers: 'What do you mean? When you say, 'peace be with you' – sometimes piously, sometimes glibly – what do you mean '*peace be with you?*'

Peace cannot be otherwise than *with you* because it is *in you*. Peace requires *action* – the action of changing The Field. The action required to change The Field takes place within you as individuals and as groups. Seek the Light within and you become peace-makers because you generate that vibration as your signature-vibration on this level and more people will be attracted to you and you can then give to them the way of peace by instructing them, teaching them how to go within and discover it. And in time you will find, as you come out of your meditations for peace, that you will no longer pick up the worries that you have left by the door. Why pick them up when peace is an absolute within you? Why worry about *anything*?

There was a time when there was peace, there was a time on Earth when the people on Earth tapped into God's vibration of peace and harmony – another word for peace. Peace is harmony – the two are interchangeable, the two are the same thing. There was a time when harmony was the underlying, the dominant vibration that fed this level before The Fall; before mankind changed the polarity of The Field. That peace has not gone anywhere, it is still within you but it is masked and I want you to think for a moment about the word 'illusion'. I describe The Field as an illusion – it *is* an illusion, it is trickery, it is simply a layer of deception that masks your true

131

inheritance, your true nature. You have to return to that period of peace, it is vitally important.

Your world, under the oppression of the illusion, is *dying*. It is running out of energy. You talk about your oil reserves, your petrol reserves, but these are physical manifestations of what is happening to the globe on a spiritual level. *The globe cannot sustain itself much longer*. You draw on its energies but do not replenish them and I am talking here *spiritually* and not materially. You take from this world everything: breaths of air, the construction of your houses, the fruits and vegetables, the animals. You take... and you take... and you take... and you take... and you draw these things into the illusion, which is negatively charged, thinking that the world has an infinite supply of spiritual energy. Michael knows how depleted he becomes after working spiritually because his life-force has been drained in order for us to communicate and needs replenishing. Imagine that that is happening on a global level; consider that every day the world is being drained of its life-force, which is not being replenished, and you see the need for peace on Earth and peace within the Earth.

You are running out of time, Ladies and Gentleman!

You are running out of time and I pray that the examples of how to change things within this book are considered and used because each soul that reunites itself with the God within becomes a point of Light, a point of energy for the world to combat the dominant vibrations of The Field.

My peace be with you! My existence is within a sphere – although sphere is perhaps the wrong word – is within a 'sea' of peaceful vibration. Am I at peace? No, because I am concerned about your world, about the Earth. I am concerned about the souls on the Earth – about you. I am concerned that the planet and its peoples get back on track; that they permeate, that *you* permeate, your physical reality with enough Light to sustain yourselves, to sustain the planet and to sustain a new way of thinking.

There is an urgency to what we do. We cannot (as part of you – as part of God) turn our backs on the situation and we feel on our higher vibration the effects of your dominant vibrations upon the Earth and upon each other. This is why we come back constantly to attempt to change things. There is greater urgency with us as time goes on on your level of consciousness.

You do not have an infinite number of tomorrows in which to put things right.

You have to begin *now*.

Chapter 12

You are here today – you are gone tomorrow

Joseph speaks. There is no Michael at the moment, which is an amusing thing: one minute you have someone there and the next you don't, because I have taken over part of his physicality so that I can speak to you. And on that note I would like to talk about 'here today – gone tomorrow', and that will be the subject of this chapter:

Here today – gone tomorrow.

In this chapter I want *you*, the reader, to face up to something; to admit something; to realise something: to realise that *one day you will not be here on this physical plane* – and even that is wrapping things up to soften the blow.

One day, Dear Reader, you are going to die.

So many individuals in your world, on your planet, feel that *they* will be the ones to escape the natural course of things; they will be the ones who will live forever; they will be the ones who will not get old, who will not become ill, who will not die. I have news for you:

Each of you is going to die.

You spend, in western civilisation, a great deal of your time denying that; avoiding that; pushing forwards in your lives as though you will always be here so you must always accumulate wealth, you must always secure for yourselves dwellings for the future and security for the future.

What future?

Let us strip things down to the basics: your existence here can be compared to the existence of the mayfly that lives for a day and then is no more. It is a sobering thought isn't it, and it is a *frightening* thought for you in the western world that you are going to die. Many cultures around your planet do accept this and prepare for it but you don't.

And so, in attacking people verbally or mentally, in carrying grudges, in perpetuating arguments – you do not realise that one day you will have to leave these things behind *and take the consequences of how you have acted onto another level of existence.*

What point is there in fighting over land that is not yours? What point is there in trying to accumulate as much wealth as you can when that wealth remains on a physical plane but you do not? What point is there in hating someone when all you take with you to your next stage of existence is the hatred and the effects of that hatred – effects that you have to work out of your system as a spirit before you can move onwards?

If you faced up to the fact that you are not a physical being but a *spiritual* being; if you faced up to the fact that one day you will not be here, then you would live your lives *differently*. You would appreciate the people around you because you would be aware of the fact that one day they will not be with you on a physical plane; that today is important because you may not have a tomorrow and today is the day when you should get your life in order. It is no use saying, 'I can live as I want to now and then sort things out as I grow older.' It is no use saying, 'The priest can absolve me so that I can go to Heaven spotless.' *You will not go to Heaven* – Heaven is a moving target; Heaven is a progression; Heaven is a state of mind and a state of being.

And no one can absolve you from your sins, from your transgressions, from the ways in which you have abused yourself and misused people but *you*. Ultimately God does not regard anything that you do as a sin, as a transgression.

Built into His physical universe and into His spiritual universe is a 'cause and effect' mechanism, and that mechanism allows each soul to filter out of itself that which it no longer needs so it can grow closer to God. Conversely that mechanism *restricts* souls from evolving as quickly as they could do when they act in a way that locks them into patterns of thought and of doing and of being that are not God-like. What I mean by that is that if you think in a way that attracts the lower vibrations of Creation, the lesser vibrations of Creation, the *heavier* vibrations of Creation, then those vibrations remain with you within your soul when you pass from this life to the next one and restrict your journey – your escape – into God-Consciousness.

God is 'Light'.

I want you to think about that word 'Light' – not light as in illumination but light as in *not heavy*. Do you see? Light as in *refined*, light as in etheric. God's touch is a light touch. If your touch during your time on Earth has been a heavy touch, then you take with you those vibrations. You lock them for a time into your soul because you believe they govern your responses and they are the way that you should act. You believe that it is right to be aggressive, right to be violent; you believe that it is right to condemn other people; you believe that it is right to condemn yourself. You have bought into the heavy matter of this physical sphere and then, when you move on, you take with you not the *matter* but the *essence* of the way you have acted. And the way that you have acted restricts your progress, pulls you back towards the Earth – very often, unfortunately, through a *desire to be there again*. So many souls *want* to get back; want to get back into the act; want to hate again; want to experience violence again; want to experience supposed control over people again.

And their souls, which have been surrounded by these heavy acts, these heavy molecules, are pulled back into physical incarnation. You repeat the process again but in that life you have to die again. In each successive life you have to move on and then you are pulled back into the same type of life and given opportunities to grow out of the way you have been thinking, the things you have been doing – which you don't take because you don't acknowledge that one day you are going to die.

If I gave you a stopwatch and said, 'You only have three hours left and you must prepare yourself to meet your Maker,' how would you act during those three hours? If you had sense you would try to repair some of the damage you had done, you would call on those people you had wronged and say, 'I am sorry – what can I do to make things right? Please forgive me.' If you had sense you would sit quietly during your last three hours in a chair and you would contemplate the areas in which you have got your thinking wrong and drop that thinking, because as soon as you drop a pattern of thought it is gone from you. It is as simple as that *but first you have to be prepared to do it.*

Instead you spend your lives on a daily basis saying, 'I have been hurt because of this. I am angry with this person because of that. I will never forgive that person because of what they did to me. The world should be this way according to me. The world should be that way according to me. These people need wiping out. This way of thinking needs wiping out. I am angry with my wife, with my children, with my workmates, with my world, with my politicians, with my armies... I am angry in so many ways.'

In order to change this world, you have to bring Light into it and the time to bring Light into it is during your *present incarnation*. The world is crying out for help. People, souls (although they do not know it) are crying out for help. Are you going to be the one who gives that help? If you are not, if you are not prepared to change your ways and to change your ways of thinking, put this book down now. Burn it, forget it, and re-enter the cycle of anger and upset and heavy vibration that so many souls re-enter incarnation after incarnation after incarnation.

My message to you is that you cannot leave the changing of the world to other people; you cannot say, 'It is nothing to do with me. The war on the other side of the world is nothing to do with me. The disaster that occurs half a world away is nothing to do with me.'

It is everything to do with you!

You are an infinite and equal part of God's Creation. What you think, how you act, affects others and affects yourself – your physical wellbeing, the wellbeing of others. My message is that it is part of you, it is *your* responsibility.

Other books may tell you that great changes are coming (and they are) but this book tells you it is time for you to stand up and be counted and be the one who realises that there is a different way to act and to live and to think and to *be...* and it is you who puts that different way into operation.

The enlightened teachers that have been sent to you were not aware that they were enlightened teachers when they incarnated. At some stage in their existence (prompted by the God within) they said to themselves, 'It might as well be me. It is a hard path, it is a dangerous path, I will meet with opposition, people will think that I am insane but it might as well be me.' And, at that moment, when they said *it might as well be me*, the purpose of their soul flooded their physical

138

body and mind: they *knew* what they had to do and what they had to say.

Each of you can be an enlightened teacher – in a small way or in a big way – each of you can be a worker for the Light by allowing the God within to take over your actions. That does not mean that you will lose your personality, that you will become a different person, that your personality will disappear; quite the opposite – your personality will be enhanced by what you are able to do through accessing the Light within.

You were not designed to be as you are; you were not designed to be a creature that is at the mercy of a physical universe. Your physical universe was supposed to be 'at the mercy of' you. You were not designed to be a creature who became ill. You were certainly not designed to be a creature who kills and injures his fellow man. And you might say, 'I have never killed anyone,' but you will have thought your thoughts against others, you will have become angry with people, you will have put down people, you will have judged people, and, in doing so, in microcosm you create the trends within The Field of conscious existence that perpetuate war, crime, illness, misery, depression. I am handing you, as you read this book now, a light – it is a lighted torch. I am asking you if you have the courage to hold that torch high and to live by example?

All the methods I have given you – the meditations to make you aware of your potential as a spiritual being, can be drawn on to create a different perspective on life and to allow you to send that perspective into The Field to change it.

Many of your businesses, your corporations, your endeavours, your personal plans, do not come to fruition because they are based on dead energy. What I mean by that is that any enterprise has to be imbued with Light before it can be successful. Otherwise there is just the idea. Without the Light behind the idea its existence in The Field is a fleeting one. What you have to do is to put Light into your every endeavour; is to create and be successful from the God-Centre outwards. If you are businessperson and you are creating a business, create that business to entertain and sustain you, yes, but as its basis let there be the Light of God and it will be successful. Not only will it be successful but every company it touches and every person it touches will receive an amount of Light by being associated with it.

If you wish to be successful as an individual – perhaps you wish to be a singer or a show-jumper or a sportsperson – do those things for the glory of God; not in a religious way but by bringing into your professionalism and into what you do the Light from within. Then you will succeed and you will touch the people around you and spread that Light to them. If you are writing a letter to a friend put Light into it; let your words come from within. Do not bother them with what is wrong in your life but ascertain what is right in your life and how much you love them and you will spread Light to them. You will see the different way of life that I am suggesting you begin to live.

Many spiritual projects also fail because they do not truly come from the heart, do not truly come from God. I am *telling you* – not suggesting to you – *telling* you that there is only one way to change this world and that is to *actually do something spiritually*. You cannot read a book, put it away and say, 'That was very nice and now I will continue with my life as it was.' There has to be change, there has to movement and motion in order for this world to get back to the state that it was once in: a paradise.

Please consider what is being offered to you: a different way of life that is nothing to do with religious fanaticism but everything to do with the God you are a part of and who created you; who asks you simply to bring Him, His knowledge, His approach, into everything that you do; who asks you to understand that life is eternal – but not here – that this is one passage, one section, one chapter in an ever unfolding book; who asks you to realise that, and who has said through the prophets: 'Live each day as though it is your last' – because it may well be. And you should not put off until tomorrow the Light that you can bring into this world day.

I tell you: you are running out of tomorrows.

You are running out of tomorrows! The world at the moment, The Field that encapsulates the world, is running mostly on hollow, dead energy. This is why your schemes fail; this is why your banks find themselves in such dire situations – because they do not put God into their ventures. They do not consider God; they create a view of *needing matter* and their projects are based on the acquisition of matter and nothing else. What about the acquisition of peace, what about the acquisition of Love, what about the acquisition of spiritual knowledge? All these things are missing from the matrix, from The Field at this time.

I would ask you, finally, to be brave enough to sit quietly by yourself surrounded by angels and to realise, to admit that which you do not admit…. that you are going to die. This is nothing to fear; this is a process that takes you closer to God and into a far better state of being (if you have lived you life in a progressive way). Admit it to yourself then think of the consequences of that truth. Think of the consequences of that truth on the people around you.

Also consider that you do not know *when* you are going to die. You may be an older person reading this or a young person and there will be suppositions. If you are old you will think: 'Well, maybe I am going to die soon.' If you are young, you will think: 'I have years and years and years left.'

Not so.

If God decides to terminate this phase of your existence He will not respect your age or your personal opinion of when you should die. You do not know when you are going to die and how much time you have left in which to change things.

So, in your meditations, look at how you can change things in your life. How can you put things right? Are there people you should be speaking to that you haven't spoken to? Are there situations where you are nurturing hurts still that need to be let go of? Is forgiveness needed in areas of your life – both for yourself and for other people? Do you approach your work correctly or your relatives correctly?

Ask yourself these questions and then determine, please, to put Light into everything you do, into all your dealings – to put God into all your dealings. And view whatever you do as *temporary*. The motive behind what you do isn't temporary, but what you do *is*. One day your job will be ashes. One day the world-encompassing corporation that you work for will be ashes. One day your house, your street, your village, will be ashes – because all these things are temporary constructs of matter and they must change. But the essence of your job, the essence of that corporation, the effects and the ramifications of having been in those situations are taken with you. Those are the permanent aspects, so you have to make sure that the permanent aspects that go from this world to the next world are of the right vibration. Otherwise you might spend centuries chipping away at the solidifications that you have created around your soul that you will wish you hadn't. If your motive is one of Love, one of progress spiritually, then you have nothing to fear. If you hate, if you cannot forgive, if you harbour a grudge, if you are angry, if you are violent, then you have *something to fear*: either because those dominant thoughts will draw you back into another incarnation where the same things will happen, or because you will realise what you have done and will have to put things right before you can move on.

Take responsibility – that is what I and the other spirits who come to talk to you ask you to do. *Personal responsibility*! No one can wash away what you have got wrong except you. No one can put things right in this world except you because the world you see is a projection of your inner world.

Take responsibility.

Be brave.

If you do not do it now you will have to do it in some future time but the world needs your help *now*.

May God bless you for considering what I have said. May God stir in you the feelings that will lead you to change. May God direct you into the circumstances that will allow you to grow and to leave behind that which is no longer of use to you.

Chapter 13

Are you moving or standing still?

Michael's notes. *Joseph* begins this chapter by answering a question that some of you may have considered in reading his books, and that is: do I see and am I influenced by *Joseph* at other times – i.e: when we are not sitting specifically for a *Joseph* communication? The answer to that is 'yes'. Sometimes I can be doing something as mundane as shopping and *Joseph* will tune in with a concept he wishes to get across to us. Before a *Joseph* trance demonstration he pops in to let me know he will be there (which is a relief!), and sometimes just by us talking about him the connection is made and he appears, enthusiastic as ever and ready to deliver new information. Sometimes I have to politely and respectfully ask that he come back at another time, which I hate to do, but there are certain everyday circumstances where to say to the people around me, 'Just a moment, I'm receiving a message from a discarnate soul who wants to save the world and once lived in Atlantis,' is not quite the thing to do! Here, then, is chapter 13, the title of which was impressed on me by *Joseph* a few days before we actually sat for this trance communication.

Joseph speaks. I began to speak to Michael a couple of days ago so that he had the theme of this chapter in his head and he said: 'No, *Joseph* don't come through now – this is not the right time,' and I knew it wasn't the right time but I wanted him to have that theme established in his mind so that I could expand on it when I *did* come through at this time. The theme of this chapter is 'movement'.

...Movement!

So, *Joseph*, what do you want to say about movement? What can movement possibly have to do with the book that you are writing in order to change consciousness on Earth?

I usually start with some statement to shock you or to shake you and the statement is this:

Many souls on Earth are standing still.

Many souls on Earth are standing still – and these are not the souls that you would expect to be standing still. I see people in your places of commerce running around, leaping out of bed in a morning, pushing food into their stomachs, moving on to more work, coming home late at night and feeling that they have accomplished something.

I see your politicians taking great care and expending great amounts of time and putting acres of thought into projects that they feel are right: polishing them, changing them and honing them.

I see people in pursuit of happiness who are saying: 'My life is moving on from point A to point B to point C and onwards. I am achieving things. I am accomplishing things: look at my new house! Look at where I will retire! Look at the money I have in the bank! Look at what I have achieved!'

...And then I see someone sitting in a room communicating with God and sending Light out into the world; seeing a vision of what they would like the world to be like.

In the first examples I gave to you I have to say that these people are standing still, and in the last example I have to say that that soul is *progressing*.

You measure things on Earth by the passage of time – because you are in a field that gives you the illusion of time – and by acquisition: acquisition of status, acquisition of material things, acquisition of *more*. You do not go from a small house to an equally small house – you go from a small house to a bigger house. You go from one level of employment to a more responsible level of employment. But these things are of the material field; they are necessary for the experiences that they give you but they are not of spiritual intent in most cases.

You are here, within this span of years that has been given to you, to *move* – to 'move forwards' – not just in earthly terms but also *spiritually*... look closely and you will see that, within the job you work at and within the material opportunities that come to you, there are also opportunities for you to move forwards *spiritually*. If you do not seize those opportunities, if you are just blanketed – enfolded – by the glory of the job or the glory of the material things you can acquire, then you are standing still. I am not saying that you should not enjoy your job or enjoy the material things that come to you (they come to you by the grace of God) but within them there are opportunities for you to move forwards as a soul.

You came into this world as a baby and you grew into an adult through change on a physical level – and that is when many people stop changing spiritually. They stop seeking; they ally themselves perhaps with a religion that does the thinking for them so that they do not have to contemplate anything spiritually and personally. They become involved in the glitter, in the glamour, in the opportunities that they see this world as being able to present to them: the job, the career, the acquisition of wealth. And so – from childhood to the grave – they pursue an adventure, but it is only of the physical level and they return to the spirit world in much the same state as they came into this world.

If I were to ask you at this point in your life (the point at which you are reading this book) how you feel you have progressed as a soul whilst you have been here, what would you say to me? Would you stare at me blankly or would you say, 'I have a nice house'?

Useless!

Or, 'I have a position of power'?

Useless!

Or, 'I am comfortable in my old age'?

Pointless!

You should measure the success of your existence here by how you have *changed*. Change is movement and you need movement as a soul. Do you still believe at this point in your life what you believed a year ago spiritually? Do you ever question your spiritual beliefs? Do you ever question the world's ways and how you came to this point in your existence? If you do not – if you still believe what you believed a year ago – you are standing still.

You can take a plane, you can take a boat… you can circumnavigate the world, you can move in all these ways, but you are standing still as a spirit. You have been given the ability to question; you have been given the ability to think things out for yourself. I have told you how to access the heart centre to see if things ring true or not from your spiritual seat, from the seat of your God-Consciousness.

Why do you not use your mind?

Are you afraid that in questioning your religion you will be cast out into Hell? (Hell does not exist – not in God's universe; it only exists in yours – it only 'exists' within you because of the situations you place yourself in.) Do you question the ethics of the place that you work for? Do you question your own ethics, your own motives? You should! You should weekly look at your life and say to yourself: 'What have I learnt this week? How am I changed? *Have* I changed? How can I instigate change?'

Sometimes it is a good thing on the level of illusion within which you exist to get rid of things and to be brave enough to say, 'I turn my back on this physical situation. I do not need this. I no longer have a use for that,' and in doing so you will allow new opportunities to be poured into your existence that will raise your soul.

So, I am asking you to always question and to begin to use your heart-mind and your physical-mind to consider: 'is this how I want things to be?'

'Do the structures of religion around me provide answers that I am comfortable with within my soul?'

'Am I being asked through my religion, through my political beliefs, through my occupational approach to the world – am I being asked to treat people fairly, to treat people well?'

'Do the material things in my life bring me joy? Do I need them? Why do I need them?'

Ask!

Ask questions!

Awaken!

And then you will see the need for change and you will find such Love within yourself that you can pour into all of your endeavours:

into your job, into your religion, into your personal life, to change these things. You are not supposed to stand still.

The problem with your world at the moment is that it is repeating the same pattern, it is standing still and it is not evolving. You acquire more technology, you acquire better ways to destroy each other, but you are basically (on a material level within the illusion, within The Field) who you were *thousands of years ago*. Can that be right? You witness progression in your own life so how can The Field that you are a part of not change? It only changes aesthetically in the way it looks to you. You still kill each other; you still have diseases that you do not know how to treat (I must correct myself here – you *do* know how to treat them, you just will not access the knowledge from your souls).

Your world has to change. *You* have to change. There has to be movement. When you depart from this planet you will find yourself in a situation where your soul calls to you, pulls you into movement, and you will not be content to sit around – no matter how beautiful the place you find yourself in may seem. You will want to move forwards and you will realise that your moving forwards thus far, from your point of physical death to your establishment in the vibration – the sphere – that you have earned the right to be in, has been caused by the way you lived your life on Earth. You can't stand still; it is not the nature of God to stand still. It is the nature of God to 'pour forth' – a movement – and to 'gather in' – a further movement. To pour forth and gather in – eternal, infinite movement.

(*Joseph* to the group: The connection is becoming weaker – there are only so many moments that we can use Michael for before there is the break in communication.)

I want you to be unafraid of movement. Movement, of course, is change and there is the word, Joseph, that we hate the most...

Change.

There has to be change – not just change in what you do superficially; on the surface – there has to be change *within*. You cannot hold onto the same beliefs for a lifetime. If you do then those beliefs are only of the mind and not of the heart. Belief from the heart is called knowledge. Knowledge is not belief – knowledge is *knowing*. Knowledge is knowing that things change, that you change, that you are here to change.

If I could (and you will dislike what I am going to say) I would grab you by the lapels and I would shake you. I would shake you out of your complacency. I would shake you simply to introduce into your life something different that makes you see that the path you have been on is not all there is. I would shake you to shake away from you some of the vibrations that you are steeped in that cause us so much sorrow on your behalf because we see you blindly going from day to day unchanging and surrounded by illusion. The only *true measure* of your world is your perception from within – from the heart. And if you have not accessed your heart thus far in your journey, you have not changed – you are not moving.

I love to unsettle – not for the sake of it, not because I am a cruel man – but in unsettling you I change you and you begin to change yourself, you begin to change your world, you begin to move forwards (I am tempted at this point to give you a great discourse on the fact that you do not, in spiritual reality, move anywhere but I have to put things into earthly terms), you transmute and you become more than you were.

So, at the end of each day ask yourself, 'Am I moving on? Have I moved on from the morning? Have I moved on in my thoughts and beliefs?' If your thoughts and your beliefs harm anyone else in any way, shape or form then you have not. If you cannot see a spiritual side to your life *at all* and invest your total energies in materialism then you have not. If you allow yourself to be steered by man-made beliefs in the name of God – beliefs that you never question then you have not.

It is time to move on, Ladies and Gentlemen, as I must now move on to return to give another teaching in a few weeks' time.

I ask your forgiveness if I offend you in anything I have said, but I do not ask your forgiveness for putting God's point of view through to you. *Someone has to.* There is a term 'the end of days'. I hope so much that before the end of your days individually you will have absorbed Light by looking at things in a different way – in a God way. And I hope and pray that we can influence enough people so that 'the end of days', meaning *the end of your civilisation*, is not just put off – the prospect of it (which is closer down the road than you think) – is not just put off but is eliminated.

You have a lot to do.

Chapter 14

How to stop 'The Field' slowing you down
(with associated questions and answers)

Joseph speaks. Good morning to you all! I have been preparing Michael, though he has not been aware of it until this point, for a week to ten or eleven days prior to this chapter to inspire him on the theme I want to talk about. It is apt that at this time Michael is tired as it is coming to the end of your year (*Michael*: we were sitting for this information as Christmas approached) and he feels that his energies are below par. I want to talk about tiredness. I want to talk about lack of achievement and I want to talk about 'the drag of The Field'.

A strange word '*drag*', but an appropriate one, as every intention on Earth is accompanied by a slowing down effect from The Field. The noblest of intentions are attacked either directly by The Field or indirectly by The Field. We have talked about the direct effect of The Field on the human psyche, on the human soul, but not about the *indirect effect*. The indirect effect of The Field on the soul is to slow down its abilities. You see, as souls we are limitless – absolutely limitless; whatever we can imagine we are capable of we *are* capable of. But, unfortunately, working against you, working against those who would be creative on the Earth plane, you have the binding effects, the slowing down effects, of The Field, which make you tired. You are not designed to run out of energy. You run out of energy because you are being fed by the energy from The Field rather than by

God-Energy. You therefore have to spend half of your time in an unconscious state so that your soul can be fed by God-Energy to keep you animated during your waking moments.

Each great creative quest on Earth has, running alongside it, if you will, the 'demons of The Field' – slowing it down, pulling on it, dragging on it. If you go into space an object keeps moving because there is very little drag against it but on Earth you cannot keep moving, there cannot be infinite movement because the Earth slows people down; The Field slows people down.

What can you do about this? Many people decide that, because their efforts take such hard work, they shouldn't bother: 'Why should I bother to change things? Why should I bother to change myself? Why should I have aspirations? Why should I have goals?' And they stop, very often quite early in their lives, wanting to achieve, wanting to change, wanting to help. It goes without saying that this is a very negative attitude! If only you understood (And you *will* understand from this point onwards, because I am now going to tell you how to do it!) that if you surround your projections into The Field with God-Energy they have far more power. For example, it is not enough to *want* people to stop fighting each other, you have to instead pray, seeing in your mind's eye a time when people stop fighting each other and seeing that time as being *now*, and then you have to surround that thought before you let it go out into the ether and out into The Field with the white Light of God-Energy. Lift the thought up; see the thought becoming more noble than the place that it is trying to affect, than The Field you are trying to put it into. Lift it up. See it ennobled, enriched; see it *Christ-ed*; see it become a beautiful, unchanging, permanent image of white Light. And then let it go; see it melt away from you. Give it to the universe – and in doing so it is as though your thoughts have gone out into space. There is less drag; The Field cannot affect them nearly so much.

In your personal endeavours with the things that you wish to accomplish in life, it is not enough to just see them as being there in the future. You need to surround them, you need to feed the thought or the thought will die. Do you understand that? You need to feed the thought that you have created with the right kind of energy in order to perpetuate it and so you have to bathe that thought in the highest vibration of Creation, which is the white Light (actually it is not white, it is a transparent quality of light but you cannot pick that up with your human receptors – with your eyes, with your mind – it does not register, so the nearest thing to it we can describe to you is white Light). Surround your thoughts of the things you want to happen with God-Light, which is the same as dedicating them in God's name, and in doing so you give them power.

Thoughts, of course, *have* power – as we have discussed earlier and in the first book – but the dominant thoughts on Earth are fed by The Field and not by God-Light, which is why the people who work for good seem to have to work so hard to make any difference whatsoever. If you want something in life, if you want it badly enough, then you can have it (if it does not affect others adversely and if it is in line with your karmic mission on Earth). However, it is not enough to just see that thing in your mind. That is only the first step. The second step is to irradiate that thought with God-Energy. By doing that you use the God that is within you to animate that thought, to give substance to that thought, to give power and longevity to that thought so that it can be pulled into being on a material level.

So, what I am saying to you, very definitely, is that **you can change your world** and that if you have failed before, if you are reading this book and saying, 'Well, I have tried to make people stop killing each other, I have tried to heal people, I have tried to end arguments, I have tried to be a peace maker and a peace bringer and nothing seems to have happened,' you have now been given the ammunition so that you can start again and this time make a real difference. Each day you can start again and you can work against the drag of The Field by bringing into your thoughts God–Energy, which is eternal, which never becomes corrupted. With the energies that you put into thoughts, if you surround thoughts with God-Energy, if you permeate them with God-Energy, you are tapping into something that cannot be degraded by The Field, in the measure that you believe it and see it in your mind's eye.

So, you now have the ammunition to change the world, you have the ammunition to heal people, and that is how Jesus healed people. He said, 'I and the Father are One,' and by doing that he identified his soul with the essence of the Father, with the highest vibrations of the Father, and brought into his vision of healing people that vibration that is everlasting. Therefore his vibration became the dominant vibration in the image of that person, stronger than the image the person held of themselves, and when that image that Jesus held of the person as being healed was superimposed over the image the person held of themselves, it became the dominant image. That image of perfection and healing changed that person in an instant from their held image – which was a weak image controlled by The Field – to a perfect image, and they were healed.

I am trying to show you that you can replace the drag of The Field with a momentum; you can give your thoughts momentum, you can give them power, creative power. In order to change your world they need that creative power – otherwise they are fed by The Field and The Field eventually makes all images created from its power fail. That is the intention of The Field. The *intention* of The Field! So you have to identify with a different intention, a God-Intention, and God intends to give you everything you want in the measure that you believe that it is true and identify with Him in co-creating it.

Your words, the things that you say to people, can be imbued with God-Light, and that is a true blessing. Even when you say 'Good Morning' to someone, if you imbue that Good Morning with the highest vibration as it comes out from you and goes towards another then your *Good Morning* has power, your *Good Morning* has healing. Anything that you say, anything that you think towards others in the name of God and in the name of good can be creative and healing in the measure that you imbue those words, those thoughts, those images with God-Power, with God-Light. You send out those images to people and they switch a light on in their souls; they turn the Light on in their souls, in their minds, so that they can see clearly, so that they can change their lives positively. Remember that *one* thought that is imbued with God-Power is worth a million words and a thousand million thoughts of others who are trying to change things based on energy that is being drawn from The Field.

The Field makes you grow old – do you realise that? The Field makes you grow old, not God but the effect of The Field instructing your cells to grow old. Therefore, if you wish to remain here (because that is *your* choice) for a long time during your present incarnation, you have to see yourself – you have to see an image of yourself – that is perfect and then surround that image of yourself that is perfect with a bubble of God–Light. You are then instructing yourselves from within God's Creation and not The Field's destruction, The Field's degradation, so you can extend your health, your life, your time here, your ability to create by enveloping everything that you do in God-Light.

You needn't be as tired as you feel at times. You certainly needn't be as depressed as you feel at times, as weak as you feel at times, as powerless as you feel at times. The reason for all these things is because you are being fed by an anti-energy, you are being fed by an energy that is finite. Even the best of intentions on this level is finite unless it is imbued with God-Power, so any construction that you put together on this level, be it a relationship – because you will eventually move on from that relationship when you go to the spirit world and leave a partner behind – or a business undertaking, will end. Look at your planet's business undertakings and you will say, 'You're wrong. *Joseph*. This company has existed for a hundred years.' Yes, but it will go soon, won't it? How many business undertakings have been on

Earth for a thousand years? How many concepts have held for a thousand years? On the whole concepts – relationships, businesses, concepts of healing – are fed by The Field, so they have built into them a finite amount of days before they degrade beyond the point of their original conception, beyond the point that the original conception can maintain itself.

I am saying to you that if you brought God into your business dealings, into your noble concepts, then they would last for a thousand years, for a million years, because you would be bringing God-Energy into them. Now this does not bode well for conventional religions, does it? It does not bode well because your religions are not able to maintain themselves in a constant form. They crumble. They degrade. They may have been around for thousands of years, yes, but they have no power and many of your concepts on Earth seemingly still exist, but are actually nothing more than empty shells – be they religions, or relationships, or businesses, or governments, or the structure of countries – they exist purely through the negative momentum of The Field. They perpetuate themselves only on the surface but inside they are dead. Any concept that is dead within is no-thing on a spiritual level and must eventually crumble.

We are, hopefully, working towards a time when you will establish on Earth concepts of right, of peace, of spirituality that will last as long as this planet lasts. How wonderful that will be! For souls to be born here into a peace-loving, God-loving, soul-loving society that does not place on them the stresses that your present society does, that nurtures them and rears them in an atmosphere where they are aware, from the time they can understand, that they are part of God and part of the universe and part of a society that can reach out to the other members of God's society on other worlds.

Other worlds exist. It is not that they do not want to contact you… they *cannot* contact you because their vibration and your vibration are so radically different; their concepts and knowledge are so different from the things that you understand. They do not keep away, they are already *here* because everything is *here* and everything is *now*. You do not know how to communicate with them because The Field holds you back. The Field, with arrogance, tells you that you are unique in the universe, that there is life nowhere else. The Field always seeks to confine you and pull you downwards into itself, forever and ever, Amen!

The point of this book is to say that it needn't be *forever and ever, Amen*. There are glorious opportunities ahead of you as souls. Before you can contact other worlds you need to be able to contact the *Yourself within yourself*, to be able to contact others on a spiritual level, to spread across this globe the Light that heals and changes and perpetuates. Isn't that what you want? Not the job that you are doing presently; not the retirement home you believe is ahead of you. Search your soul! Isn't what you are yearning for – a different way, a different attitude, the peace that comes from knowing that you belong to God and to each other and to yourself; the peace that comes from knowing that you are transforming this world into what it should originally have been and what it *was* for a time before things became complicated? The Field is so complicated. It feeds on complication. It feeds on a million concepts it worries about and mixes together and forms barriers to truth with. The truth is simple. The truth is this: *whatever you believe singly and as a civilisation you create.*

It is time to create God's image of society for you. It is time to bring yourselves out of the darkness, out of the drag, out of the fatigue, out of the depression.

...I feel it is time to invite some questions, which can be included in this chapter if you ask the right things and so, whilst we have this link this morning, I would like to ask you if there is anything you would like to ask me?

David. Yes. You imply that The Field has an *intent* – almost as if it is conscious. It wasn't always this way, was it? Before The Fall it wouldn't have been this way, would it?

Joseph. There is a consciousness to everything. If I reach out with Michael's hands and touch the air, he perceives the air as being separate from himself, but it isn't because there is only ultimately one field, **there is only one consciousness.** Existing within that consciousness is the consciousness of The Field that originally was an area of life – nothing more – an area of God that contained souls, and those souls and that consciousness were in harmony with everything else. Shutters came down within the consciousness of the souls living within The Field when The Fall took place. Shutters from within! All that I am attempting to do is transform people from within. There is no way that The Field can be transformed from without because the mistake lies within the consciousness of those souls that were involved; were trapped within The Fall. I know that sounds like a paradox but the key to changing this world comes from within because The Field can only change when the souls that are radiating a view of that field change themselves. So, yes, The Field has a consciousness, but everything has a consciousness. What I am trying to do is re-establish God-Consciousness, God-Awareness, within the souls within The Field so that The Field changes. Do you understand that?

David. Yes.

Joseph. If you could see things from my point of view, which you cannot do with your earthly eyes (though you can when you return to us at night) you would see that we are like cells within an intelligence, within a brain, if you like – although that is so poor an analogy that I have to change it! …We are like atoms within Creation. We cannot be separated from that Creation but we think ourselves to be individuals and separate. There is only one Creation; it folds in on itself and yet it is limitless. How can I describe things that do not work well with words? …It is infinite and yet it includes everything within itself. There is just one consciousness but so many ways of viewing that one consciousness from the viewpoint of the 'individual' souls.

This is the great problem we have in convincing people that do not want to be convinced that they are not separate but are a mirror reflecting a part of that consciousness. They struggle against that concept as though it is something perverse but despite their objections the concept is a truth. *We are part of the Universal Consciousness.* The mirrors within The Field that are the 'individuals' (or the illusion of individuals) have become clouded, have become smoky; they do not reflect the true creative consciousness – only a portion of it. They cannot be brought back to full God-Consciousness except by volition, however. They have to *want* to come out of the darkness – every soul!

Whilst there are still souls in the darkness, the other souls are not completely reflecting God-Consciousness again because we are all One. Even we on the spirit levels feel a heaviness at times, albeit it to the most infinite degree, because we are linked to you, and what happens at any one point within Creation affects the rest of Creation. We are not saying that The Fall affects worlds that are distant from you and other vibrationary realities to the effect that it affects you but it is there, it is part of the consciousness and it is a part of the consciousness that needs to grow and blossom again to lift up the Whole.

For this reason people, souls, cannot really opt out. They cannot say, 'This is nothing to do with me.' Of course it is! If you turn your back on humanity you turn your back on yourself; if you are cruel to humanity you are cruel to yourself.

Personal responsibility! The key to what we are trying to achieve is to first of all make you aware that you are personally responsible, that you have a link to everyone else in your world. You cannot escape that link. You cannot close your front door and say, 'I am not now linked to everyone.' Of course you are – you cannot be otherwise. It is only your perception that is providing misinformation. This is why we come back – we cannot in conscience do otherwise. Every soul on Earth is our responsibility. I am not talking in terms of the decisions that others make, I am talking in terms of realising that what you do affects every other soul. *Every other soul.* Everywhere!

So, you have to make your choices carefully, spiritually, lovingly, harmoniously. This is what I mean by it being your responsibility, because if there is only you, then everything you do affects the rest of you. A strange paradox but everything you do affects this universe; the *whole* universe. Every thought you create affects the physical universe and every thought that everyone else creates affects the universe and you are all you, but there are very different thought processes emanating from the different aspects of you within the now. Careful thought, careful choices, meditation – so that you can connect with the higher side of life, with the higher molecules of existence – these are the things we are trying to bring through to you, to suggest to you. Otherwise your world will not change except to degrade, and you don't want that or you would not be reading this book.

Do you have another question?

Jane. I have one – it is something that perhaps needs clarifying. I wasn't sure whether we as mankind had co-created the Earth? I got the impression from previous lectures that we had co-created the Earth rather than God or angels making it. I wondered, if that was the case, why we don't understand how the physical world works if we actually co-created the rocks and the trees and bodies and everything in the first place?

Joseph. You do understand. *You do understand!* Your purpose on a spiritual level during your life is to *remember* who you are and you *do* have that memory of the time when you were other than what you appear to be now. Your present form is a compression of what you were, what you still are. It is a consolidation, a heaviness, a heavy representation of what you once were and will be again. You are compressed into The Field, you are limited by The Field – or you feel that you are. If you are a part of God (which you are) then you create. You create *today*. You create the rocks and the trees and the sky *today* because you put into them, by your view of how your life is, how *they* are. So your trees eventually decay. They decay more slowly than you do because you give them less thought than you give yourself. Your rocks decay but they decay more slowly than you do because you give them less thought than you give yourself, but you are, nevertheless, creating what happens to them. You say to yourselves, 'It is a miserable day.' Singly and en masse you say, '*It is a miserable day*' and, by saying that, it *becomes* a miserable day. You place into the day your expectation of it and you affect the molecules of Creation that you placed there in the first place.

You are no different now than you were when you were 'individualised' from God, when you set out on the great journey and the great adventure. The difference lies in how you perceive your ability. Day after day you say to yourself, 'I cannot do this', 'I am unworthy of that', 'There is no way I can achieve this or that or the other' and so you maintain the barrier between you and your God-Creativity. You believe that you cannot create, therefore you cannot create, but you are creating the belief that you cannot create! You are proving to yourself that you are God-like by creating your inability to create. It is what you have chosen out of the ether.

It is dangerous for you to understand that you can create without wanting to create the right thing, so there has to be a step to redeem the Earth, a step to uplift the Earth. There first has to be an education spiritually – not religiously, but *spiritually* – to make you aware that you are Light, to make you aware that you are a creative being, to make you aware of your responsibility to others and to yourself and then to add to that your ability to create so that you can create a different society. Do you see that? Do you fully understand that?

Jane. Yes. I just wondered who, in the first place, decided that there would be rocks and trees, etc?

Joseph. You needed a plane of reference. Out of the *'no-thing'* had to come *'some-thing'* so that you could experience. All life seeks to experience, to experience infinite variety, infinite permutations. Your strata of the world acts as a backdrop against which you play out your perceived physical lives.

If you are asking why is your planet of a certain type, why does it have the structures that it has, it is part of Creation. God creates and then, within that Creation, within what He has created, *you* create because you are God. You are the Whole and you are the 'individual' at the same time; you are the dot within the circle. So, as you reach out across a planet you, through your thoughts – as I have just said – through your beliefs, create that planet. You create the way that it looks, you create the way that it behaves. It cannot be otherwise. You are constantly saying *'This is our world.'* Therefore you are maintaining it – even now in its present state.

So there is no difference – it is a metaphysical question but there is no difference – between God creating the universe and you creating the surface of the planet or you creating a society. It is the same thing. Which is more powerful, God as the Whole or God as an 'individual'? There is no difference. There is no 'individual'. Ultimately there is no Whole, there is just Creation and here we are getting closer to what God (as we perceive Him) is: Creation bringing forth from the nothing the something and constantly reworking the something into something else. Experience; sense; adventure – these are the things that are God-like… to bring forth always new scenarios, new vistas, new ways to experience but always to Love, always to adore and cherish all aspects of what has been created.

This is where you differ from God-Mind. You lost that path of cherishing, of nurturing, of loving, and then it became your creation.

So your creation now, from your viewpoint as a pocket of God-Consciousness, your creation is skewed.

Do you now see where freewill comes into the equation? God has to let God be. Therefore, you can only associate with the greater Creation through your own choice; otherwise God will be going against Himself, Creation against Creation. So we can suggest, we can illuminate, we can lead, we can guide, but we cannot *force*. In order for you to experience the greater God, the God beyond The Field, the unrestricted God, *you* have to decide to do so.

This is where this book differs from other books. This book does not tell you that everything will be all right. It won't unless *you* decide it will. This book does not tell you that some greater God will take care of things. Yes, He will, but first you have to reach out to Him in consciousness. You are God. You are creating this world. It is time for you to create something else, something that is in tune with the Love of Creation. When you do that, creative Love flows through you and your structures are perpetuated. Do you see?

Jane. Yes.

Joseph. I am tiring Michael. Is there a final question?

Jane. There is just one thing... going back to The Fall, there seemed to be some God-men and some ordinary men, but the God-men were the ones that changed the vibration and I wondered what the difference between the God-men and the ordinary people was?

Joseph. You were *all* God-men and women and children. You could not be otherwise. There was a hierarchy – although that is a difficult term and is not quite what I mean. At first there were certain beings that were tasked with creating the backdrop of life, tasked with maintaining the status quo within which the other spirits could experience. There was then a shift in consciousness that affected the whole pocket of God-Consciousness. What if I were to suggest to you that the whole of mankind is also an individualisation of God? That you exist as an 'individual' soul (and yet you do not, because you are God) but you exist also within a greater sphere of consciousness that is an 'individual' consciousness (and yet isn't, because it is part of God). What I am saying to you is that you are all part of a particular 'block' of consciousness, a particular vibration of consciousness, a particular projection of consciousness.

So, although there was a hierarchy and decisions were made, because you are part of a block of consciousness, the consequences of those decisions applied to you all. Consider group souls and how they appear to be individual members and yet can operate as a whole. It is no different – imagine the population of the Earth as a complete group soul. So, the dominant vibrations affect the Whole. When decisions were made which affected the vibrationary signature of the world adversely (and this took a long time, a *long* time) it sort of sneaked up on people. When those decisions were made, those decisions affected not only the decision-makers but everyone else as a single conscious projection of God.

It is not that certain souls are being punished for something they did not do. No one is being punished; it is simply the structure of Creation that relates to your bond of consciousness that means that the decisions affected the Whole, encased the Whole, imprisoned the Whole. The Whole has to move on, which is why things change, apparently, so slowly on your level. You must stop thinking in terms of crime and punishment; you must stop thinking in terms of justice and injustice. You have to think in terms of a separation of consciousness through decisions that were made that had consequences and that the rest of Creation is trying, attempting (succeeding too, we have to say, for we cannot think otherwise) to absorb back into its greater consciousness that area of 'out-of-step' consciousness that was created as a result of The Fall.

I have to stop now because Michael is depleted for much the same reason that I have been talking about today – the drag of the physical world and the demands of the physical world.

The Trilogy.

There is not long to go now before this second title is completed, and then the third title – which looks at our areas of life, our reality (*Michael*: here *Joseph* is referring to the spheres of 'reality' he and other spirits exist in) – will be far different again than many of the books that have been written on the subject. It will not paint a rosy picture of Heaven but will instead concentrate on the continued journey of the soul, the choices that are open to the soul and, again, the consequences of actions on Earth taken into a different vibration.

So the three will come together to show you what is wrong, to show you how to put it right and to show you the effects of not putting it right when you return to the higher consciousness. Between the three books there should be enough momentum for people who consider these things to make changes.

It feels to me like I am sometimes 'bullying', but if I do not unsettle people there is no point to the books. *I have to unsettle.* You have to lever the barnacle away from the side of the ship so that the barnacle can go with the stream and can anchor itself somewhere else. If it is comfortable it will remain there forever in the fetid water. I have to unsettle people, there is no other way. To lift them up, yes, but you cannot praise them for getting things wrong, you cannot say, 'There, there – it's all right,' because it isn't.

A difficult task and a difficult message – and a difficult message to take in because many people have so much ego that they do not want to be told that there is anything wrong, and certainly they do not want to be told that they can take control of their own lives and change them; it is so much easier to allow everyone else to do that.

Thank you for listening to me.

Chapter 15

You change the world

Michael's observations: And so the second *Joseph* book, with this communication, drew to a close. *Joseph*'s communications would continue without a pause, however, as he immediately began to channel information for his third book, which he mentions here. At this time we were in the early stages of considering public trance meetings at which *Joseph* would take me over, invite questions and speak to attendees directly. These meetings would go on to become a regular part of our lives from this point onwards, and *Joseph*'s comments when asked if he would consider addressing such gatherings are included at the bottom of the chapter.

Joseph speaks. It is appropriate that you have been talking about the camera you have set up today (*Michael*: a reference to our new camcorder, used here to film a session for the first time), because this is the final chapter of my second book and it is by far the most important chapter, because this book has been concerned with what you can do – *what you the reader can do* – to change this world for the better. I refer to the camera because the camera records images and, each time you play back those images, you relive the circumstances that have been imprinted into the technology – until you wish to delete them, to get rid of them.

The most important thing you can do to create a new world is *to see it*, is to make your own 'films', your own 'movies', of the world you wish to see in your mind's eye.

(*Michael*: *Joseph* next describes some meditational suggestions and options to enable you to do this. To practise any one of these please slowly enter into your usual relaxed state then follow *Joseph*'s visualisations.)

So – you might begin by visualising a world that is at peace. You could imagine cities and towns that are at peace, where people are smiling at each other as they go about their business and where there is no violence. In your mind's eye you could take yourself through a day of what it would be like to live in such a city, where you can go into a shop or a café and sit down in harmony with other people; where you can feel their blessings and their Love towards you; where you can work in harmony with your colleagues; where the car drivers do not become agitated by the pressure they normally feel in this world; where no-one becomes fatigued because they are working within their spiritual capabilities, and where money is not 'God' but joy of life and joy of being is 'God'. So, you could create such a scenario in your mind and see – create – a city like that.

Then you could store that 'film' in your memory, so that you could access and replay it on a daily basis, and next create a different image of a world at peace: this time seeing different countries at peace. You could look to the troubled areas of your world and become a director of your own 'film' wherein those troubled areas are at peace; where the troops have gone back to their bases; where the terrorists have dismantled their weapons of destruction and their explosives; where the two sides come together for talks that do not result in violence but in understanding and tolerance and a willingness to change. See – create – all these things in your mind's eye.

You can store that 'film' in your memory and now see a world where there is no cruelty – no cruelty to children; where children grow up with parents who truly love them and do not abuse them and are not violent to them; where children are respectful of their parents and respectful of society; where children grow in Love to become members of a society that is harmonious and based on spiritual growth.

And you can file that 'film' in your memory and go on to create many, many more.

(*Michael*: I don't need to mention the closing of chakras again at this point, do I? Good.)

…And you may say, '*Joseph*, what good is that – me imaging a world that is peaceful, a world that is how I want it to be or, *more importantly*, how I believe God wants it to be?'

As you imagine, you create.

Haven't I told you this in the first book? Haven't I told you this in aspects of this second book? As you imagine, you create. You should therefore spend some time each day sitting down to open up your 'film library', because the 'films' that you play in your imagination each day *contribute* to the changes that must come to this world.

The fruits of your imagination go out into the ether and become reality.

Do you understand that? They become reality! What I have tried to teach you in these two books is: *whatever you see and believe and feel to be true – you create*. So, instead of being shocked by the violence of your world you have to imprint the matrix of your world, the illusion of your world, The Field of your world, with a different set of values. If you only see the violence then you help to perpetuate that violence. *You!* Whether you are a worker in an office, or a retired person, or a priest, or a nurse, or a doctor or a solicitor or perhaps the most respected person of your community – no matter who you are and what you do – if you see only violence you contribute to that violence.

Therefore, you have to think in a different way if you truly wish to change this world. And it is no use hiding on top of a mountain or sealing your doors and windows and turning your back on the Earth – that is not what you are here to do. You are here to become involved with the evolution of mankind; you *are* a part of the evolution of mankind. What you choose to do with each of your days on Earth *is vitally important* – not just to your own physical evolution, but to the evolution of every man, woman and child around this globe. Therefore, if you truly want to be a champion of spiritual change, you must make choices every day that allow that change to manifest around the globe.

You have to see *the best* in people, and by that I mean that you have to get past their violence, their lust, their fear, their ignorance, to the heart of the matter, because at the heart of the matter and the heart of each person there is God. The consciousness of God is waiting to be reborn through the soul of that person, waiting to manifest itself once again, waiting to change that person completely on a physical and mental level. They cannot be changed at a spiritual level because at that point they are part of God – they are part of the dot within the circle. You have to change the physical, the mental, the projection – the projection that is born out of fear, the projection that is born out of a memory of loss – i.e. a racial memory and an individual memory of a time when you were consciously connected to God and were living in bliss and in harmony via that connection. But that connection has not been lost – it has simply been buried.

The violence in your world, the fear in your world and the destruction in your world are the product of 'children' who do not know how to act. They do not have the advice of the 'Parent' – not because the Parent has been in anyway lacking in His bringing up of those children but because they have chosen, through their past mistake, to cut off the connection to the Source, to cut off that advice, to cut off that Love and, as a consequence, they run around lost and they strike out in anger and in pain because they do not understand. It is your job, yes – *your* job, to make them understand. Not by meeting violence with violence, or fear with anger, but by connecting to them through your vision of how you should be and how this world should be. That is how you change things.

If you have read this book to this point and then put it down and forget it you are making a *grave mistake*. You need to take up your responsibility to others. You cannot opt out of being part of the human family or of the God-family. You are, at the moment you are reading this, *connected to every other soul* – not just to the souls on this world but also to the souls on the spirit levels that are migrating back to God. You cannot opt out of that; you cannot turn your back on it (through free will, yes, you can choose to do so, but it remains as a fact – a connection – within your soul). You cannot disconnect yourself from the Whole because there is only You, creating Your universe second by second.

There is only You.

Choose to create wisely. Pass on the message to other people. Instruct them on what you have learnt through the book, in the ways that they can change this world.

I have often said that the world does not change through politicians or through force; it changes through perception, it changes through creation. Imagine that you are a great artist painting a canvas of how you want your world, your living, your existence, to be. Not just for you but for everyone else. You have that creative ability. It may not show in your physical life; you may never have painted a picture, you may never have created a piece of art or a piece of sculpture, but you are creative in your *essence*. You are part of God and God creates. You have, in your imagination, therefore, to create the next step of how you wish the world to be. And you must pray before you do this to ask for clarity in the way that you wish this world to be because, as you try to create your 'films', you will find that you have prejudices, that you inevitably wish one group of people to be more peaceful than another and that there are certain reservations that you have about praying for certain people. This is because of the pollution of this world and because you are receiving information on a physical level only so you are judging.

If you truly wish to change the world you must pray for everyone from (in your view) the most innocent to (in your view) the most guilty, and, by praying for them, you change them. Remember (and this may be difficult for you to accept), that these people are a part of you; that the people who murder, the people who rape, the people who steal, the people who commit acts of mass-terrorism *are part of you*. Now that might frighten you but remember it also frightens *them* at soul-level because they realise at soul-level that you are part of them. You have to reverse the flow: instead of them bringing terrorism, bringing violence, bringing fear, bringing anger, bringing depravity to you (and you saying 'yes', *how terrible things are*), you have to reverse the flow and bring to them through your imaginings – through your reaching out spiritually from your soul – peace, Love, understanding, calmness, the warmth of God and the directives of God that will flow through you if you do what I am suggesting you do. You have to look at things in a new way.

I have mentioned in the books that time as you understand it will not bring you these opportunities forever. In a way they will, but in your current set-up, in the current set up of society, they will not bring you opportunities forever because *you are living on finite energy*. This is another reason why you should imagine the world as you wish it to be because, in doing so, you bring God-Energy into the world and you extend the time in which you are allowed to change. The energies that you live off physically and mentally are, for the most part, finite because they are derived from the illusion that you have created. That energy – like your resources, like your mineral oils – is running out. You cannot perpetuate the same energy; it is dissipating, it does not have the creative force that it once had because you are using it again and again and again and it is fading in its intensity.

So, if you do not introduce new energy… God-Energy – the original energy, creative energy – into this world, into the illusion, there will come a point where the illusion will not be able to sustain physical life. And at that point there will be a withdrawal, there will be a retreat and there will be (as you understand time) a great deal of time which must pass before the Earth (or a planet similar to it) is able to sustain physical life again so that you can re-enter the physical manifestation of matter in order to redirect yourselves towards God.

Love is escape; action through Love is escape. For you, initially, and then for the people that you have been praying for and have been imagining as being more God-like.

You cannot stay here! You are not supposed to stay here and you will say, '*Joseph*, I don't want to stay here. I want to move on.'

Do you?

Then you have to create the atmosphere for others that allows you to move on. During your lifetime you have to create enough God-Energy so that you can make the transition to the next levels. And you will say, 'Well, I will go to the spirit world, I will leave this place'. Yes, you will, but will your soul call you back into incarnation through your desire to be part of this illusion again? It is one thing to say with your physical mind, 'I want to leave this place,' but another thing to say with the spiritual heart, 'It is time for me to leave; I do not want to return.'

There are so many attractions to this place that pull you back into physicality. It may be that you are addicted to something you eat or some sensation ...or the chaos of the place. Many of you are attracted to the chaos of this Earth and it becomes like a drug – you emerge from one situation and you say: 'Why have I had to suffer like this?' and then you put yourself through the same situation again and again, experiencing a plunge into the situation and then some kind of resurrection into a better state of mind. You then say, 'I have come through this!' The point is that you need not have gone through it in the first place! But you repeat ...and you repeat ...and you repeat.

If I am frightening you or unsettling you then that in one way is good because it means that I have touched a nerve and it means that you will look again at the ways of extracting yourself from this illusion. My message is not one of *hope* (what good is hope?) but it is a message of *certainty*. It is a message that says: 'There is a way out.' It is a message that says: 'There is a way out for this physical level; you can change it; thousands and thousands of years of bloodshed and senseless violence can end and you, *you*, Reader, have the *power* to start this revolution and to maintain it.'

Isn't that wonderful? *You* have the power! Please do not retreat from that power. Please do not say, 'Oh, that is for someone else to make the decisions.' It is for *you* to make the decisions. God has chosen *you* to change things; to change the world. Each of you is a changer of worlds if you will only but realise it. And one day you have to realise it – whether it is today as you read this book or in a million years' time – you have to realise it. You have to come round the circle that has the dot at its centre to the point at which you began as an individual and say, 'Yes, I am a part of God. Yes, I am a creative force. Yes, I am more than this poor, grey, impoverished illusion.'

My heart bleeds for this planet and for you because the solution is so simple. The physical mind that is connected to this illusion and the illusions of need within this illusion make everything so complicated, so complex. You can escape *in spirit* from here today... now! You can help others to escape... now! You begin to change things the moment you act as I have suggested (always *suggested*, not ordered – never ordered – always suggested) that you do in these books.

It is up to you and that is the bottom line: *it is up to you!*

Immediately I complete the dictation for this book I will begin to talk about and to begin the third book. The third volume in this series concerns what will happen next... and there is a subject that many people back away from: 'I will live today and I will think about what happens after I die when I get there.'

No, you won't – not if I have anything to do with it! You will consider it, please, *now* – because in illustrating what happens to you next perhaps I can change your perception of how you should be relating to this world *now*.

So, the third book will take you on a journey into other spheres of reality, into other spheres of spiritual evolution. I will demonstrate, as much as I am able, how you will live, the things you will be capable of, the environments you will find yourself in, the tasks you will be able to undertake, how the journey will streamline and change you into what you originally were.

And so, Dear Angel reading this book, farewell until the next book. Please, not for me but for *you*, consider what I have said; not for me but for *others* consider what I have said; not for me but for the *poor world* that is weary of supporting a race that only seeks to destroy it consider what I have said... and by the time we meet again in the written word you will already have made glorious changes.

...What would you ask me before I go?

175

David. Michael wanted to know whether you would be available, *Joseph*, to lecture directly to select audiences in the future.

Joseph. It is already written that I will be.

It is set out that my involvement with the masses, with more people, with rooms full of people, will stimulate interest in the message. It is amusing to me to *become a 'celebrity'*, and your culture of celebrity makes me laugh but it is necessary. It is felt that there be a personality that exudes strength and commonsense and puts into perspective many of the attempts to bring through something meaningful from the higher spheres. There has to be a yardstick, there has to be sense, and that is why I and Michael (who has already been briefed on this – although he will not know anything about it on a physical level) are prepared to do this.

What else?

Jane. Would that become a fourth book of audience questions to *Joseph*?

Joseph. If you wish it to be. The principle message is in the three books but I will try and others will be working with me – remember that I am only a figurehead and a mouthpiece and that there are many influences that flow into my aura because I am at a stage of evolution where the separateness between souls is very much less than it is here. So I will be relaying information and answers from a great number of my companions. I will try at all times, whilst having to work within the confines of the Earth plane (which is difficult for me), to bring through deep or – *extensive* is a better word – answers to the questions that are asked of me. So, in the measure that that is important information then, yes, it would be acceptable and a fine idea for that to be produced as a book or in some way made available to people who cannot come to see one of the meetings where we will manifest.

I should warn you to warn people that there may be phenomena at these meetings because the amount of power that is required to sustain trance energies to a room full of people often means that the barriers between your world and ours are thinned to the extent that there will be manifestations. But that should promote your cause – that should give more credence to the fact that I am not Michael but someone speaking through him. So you may have from one corner of the room lights or noises or other phenomena that will perhaps alarm people …but so be it. We exist. We do not hide the fact that we exist and it will no doubt allow the publicity surrounding such meetings to spread more rapidly.

One more question then I must go.

David. Nothing from me, thank you.

Jane. No, nothing from me.

Index

A
abundance 27, 64, 65, 66, 67, 69, 70
Atlantean 20
Atlantis 21, 22, 108, 144

B
Band of Light 12, 58
belief 28—31, 49, 63—66, 70, 73, 150, 162

C
chakras 48, 87, 96—97, 120, 169
     head chakra 91
change 149
channelling 34
children 31—32, 35—36, 42—43, 46—47, 52, 57, 65—66, 68, 70,
75, 80, 87, 98, 105, 113, 116, 137, 164, 169, 170—171
     brought into this world 125

encourage their dreaming 31
conscious mind 25, 27
    expectation of life being miserable 43
Creation 35, 37, 47, 55, 69, 73, 74, 82, 119, 136, 138, 154, 156, 159, 160, 162, 163, 164, 165, 171
    creating negative things as well as positive things 78
    transmute matter 90

D
demons 79, 81, 153
    you created 'demons' 79
doctrine 100, 104, 107, 110
    dogma 98, 101
dot-within-the-circle 16—17
dreams 24, 28—33, 73, 85
    depravity 25
    disease 25
    greater dream 27—28
    heading for cataclysm 32
    lack 25
    loss 25
    of violence 25
    only means of expressing existence 24
    the dreamer is not the dream 24
    wrong dream 25

E
Earth 22
    destruction 22
    Earth plane 41, 62, 126, 152, 176
    Earth requires Light 88
    problem with 25
    pulls at you 82
    The Earth is dying 88
enlightened teacher 138—139

entities 75—77, 79, 80—81, 91
    from the lower levels 91

F

fear 43, 48, 53, 57—58, 60, 62—65, 68, 72—74, 76—77, 79—81,
88, 94, 110, 120, 128, 141—142, 170—172
    soul externalises its fears 73
free will 122, 171

G

ghosts 60
    ghost-hunting 60
God 17
    a circle 17
    breathed life into 72
    communion with 108
    contained within everything 19
    contains everything 18
    cyclic in nature 17
    does He suffer when we suffer? 45
    exists within a dream 33
    God is Love 51, 102, 109, 111
    God is not angry 77
    God is not religion 100
    God-Light 83—84, 86—88, 116, 121, 154—156
    is joyous 35
    Is there more than one God 18
    nothing outside of 18
    reunification with 115
    voice of 115
    Why does God let this happen? 36
    works slowly 121
    Godhead 70, 105
group souls 165
guides 15, 44, 93

Silver Star 93—94, 97

H

harmony 29, 68, 81—82, 110—111, 115, 117, 124—125, 131, 159, 168, 170

Heaven 57, 100, 104, 136, 166
    is a moving target 136
    You will not go to Heaven 136

Hell 147

holy men 81

I

illness 25, 43, 53, 62, 66, 87, 90, 98, 128, 139

illusion 20—21, 28, 30, 32, 47, 55, 57, 59, 60, 65, 72, 76, 78, 79, 80, 84, 88, 90, 94, 97, 106, 108, 115, 125—127, 129—132, 146, 148—150, 160, 169, 173—174, 181

imagination 56, 85, 95, 127—128, 169, 172

incarnation 41, 43, 137—138, 142, 156, 173

J

Jesus 74, 155
    I and the Father are One 155

joy 25, 27, 34—35, 37, 38—39, 40—42, 46, 67, 114, 148, 168

L

letting go 127, 128

Light 23
    into your physical and spiritual existences 23
    is God 118
    is your connection to God 118
    join together to produce 45
    power of the 80
    where you began 119

Lords of Karma 41, 46

Love 20, 25, 31, 33, 51, 52, 53, 54, 55, 56, 57, 58, 59, 63—69, 74, 77, 80, 89—90, 95, 96, 99, 101—111, 115, 117—119, 121—122, 128, 140—142, 148, 150, 163—164, 168—169, 171—173
    what is Love? 110

M
magic 94
    art of the magician 94
man 16, 21—22, 28, 36, 41—42, 52, 62, 72, 86, 100—102, 139, 150, 170
mankind 39, 49, 54, 64—65, 68, 70, 73, 84, 99, 101, 105, 108, 131, 161, 165, 170
meditation 48—49, 55—56, 81, 85, 87, 89, 94—95, 97—98, 116—119, 126—128, 161

O
Oneness 18, 110—111, 124
oppression 112—114, 117—118, 120, 130, 132
    means of trying to manifest their personal world-view 113
    mould other souls 113
    oppressing yourself 116
other planets 47

P
peace 29—30, 40, 51, 68, 78, 81—82, 110, 119, 121, 123—132, 141, 154, 157—158, 168, 172
    has a vibrational value 124
personal responsibility 142, 160
perversions 75—76, 78, 125
    a temptation from outside 78
physical mind 79, 90, 104, 173, 174
    enemy in your head 90
prayer 47, 108, 119
    has no energy 108

R

reality 16, 20, 24—25, 28, 33, 64, 70, 73, 89—90, 109—110, 112, 115—116, 132, 150, 166, 169, 175

    always a dream 28

religion 17, 22, 50, 67, 98—109, 113, 118, 146—149

    a man-made construct 101

    are illusion 55

    does the thinking for them 146

    is a blasphemy 109

    one of the greatest evils 101

    overthrown 102

    written word 102

Revelation: Joseph's Message 15—16, 49, 54, 58, 82

ritual 22, 98

running out of time 132

S

saving the world 21

society 19—21, 25, 29, 40, 44, 47, 53, 83, 101, 104, 112—113, 118, 157—158, 162—163, 169, 172

soul 16—19, 24, 27—28, 35, 44—47, 52, 63—67, 70, 73—76, 79, 81—82, 97, 100—103, 105—106, 111, 114—115, 119—120, 125—126, 129, 132, 136, 138, 142, 144, 146—149, 152—153, 155, 157—158, 160—161, 165—166, 170—173, 179

    carries around its own fears 73

    each soul is progressing 101

    many souls on Earth are standing still 145

    most lost in the illusion 79

    progressing 146

spirit worlds 19, 45, 47

    spirit spheres 39

spiritual energy 22, 48, 132

subconscious 25, 27, 58, 63—65, 69, 70, 129

T

temptation 72, 74—75, 78

The Fall 13, 35, 40—43, 47, 54, 63—64, 66, 68, 71, 79—80, 88, 108, 131, 159, 160, 164, 165

The Field

    introduction to 13

    became polluted 35

    becoming an increasingly violent field 42

    deliver to and draw energies from 70

    has developed an ego 127

    is almost anti-God 47

    is conscious 40

    makes you grow old 156

    only a dream 33

    only changes aesthetically 149

    running mostly on hollow, dead energy 141

    step outside of 40

    your thoughts contribute to 37

the mind 73, 76, 78—79, 104, 150

the third book – concerns what will happen next... 175

trance 15, 24, 34, 61, 93, 144, 167, 177

    trance medium 15

U

unconscious mind 25

universe 16

    a repeating cycle 17

    beginning of 16

    expands 19

    other universes 18

    physical 18

    spiritual universes 18

W

walls 48—49, 51, 53—55, 57—58, 60
    racial wall 50
    religious wall 50
    spiritual wall 50
    the barriers 49, 54, 57—58, 106, 109, 177
weapons 80, 83, 168
    that kill no-one 80
    that weapon is Light 83
    wield the weapon of Light 85
world 20—21, 23, 26—33, 36—37, 39—42, 44—45, 48—49, 51—52, 54—55, 57—60, 66, 70, 74, 76—79, 81—83, 86, 88, 91—92, 98, 100—103, 106—109, 112—119, 121, 125, 129—135, 137—138, 140—150, 154—156, 158—161, 163—175, 177, 181
    other worlds exist 157
    to change the world 172

Y

you are perfect 28, 29

An Audience with
JOSEPH
on DVD

See Michael channel Joseph

as he invites and answers questions from an audience in this enlightening 90-minute DVD

Here are two short excerpts from *Joseph*'s highly informative spiritual demonstration…

Q. *Joseph*, can you explain about '*The Field*' you have been referring to? What is The Field?

Joseph. To explain The Field we have to explain what you are and why originally you were here. You are *Light*. Also you are angelic – if you understand that? You talk of angels and have books about angels; you revere angels, you pray to angels. …**You are angels.**

Originally, as angelic beings you were given an area (that is an approximation in words for something I cannot build in words) – you were given an area in which to experience yourself, in which to experience other aspects of yourself. At that time you were totally aware of who you were, totally aware of your connection to God and totally aware of your ability as part of God – as God's issuing, as God's children, if you like – you were totally aware of your ability to create… (*continues*)

Q. If you were to advise us of the one thing that would have the biggest impact on raising consciousness on this planet, what would it be?

Joseph. Light! The one thing that will raise consciousness on this planet is Light; to see the Light that you have within yourself but – not only that – to see the Light that everyone else has within themselves. To recognise the Light, to ignore the darkness; in doing that you draw the Light out of others, you remind them of who they are, you set alight that soul-path that is constantly calling to them but they cannot usually hear it…

You might say that the one factor that is missing from this world is love. The two are interchangeable, the two are the same thing: Light is Love; Love is Light…(*continues*)

Band of Light
MEDIA

To order this and future DVDs visit:
www.josephspeaks.com

Also available
REVELATION: JOSEPH'S MESSAGE
...A book to change your world

Joseph, the highly evolved spirit guide, has lived many times on Earth and is deeply concerned about the state and fate of the world. Speaking through the mediumship of Michael G. Reccia, *Joseph* now returns with his vital message for mankind.

In this first book of the series, *Joseph* invites you to understand who and what you really are, where you came from, why you are here and the miraculous things you are capable of achieving. Offering a completely different way of looking at life, *Joseph* reveals the amazing potential of the human spirit and provides a plan for changing the future of this planet before it's too late.

Intelligent, thought-provoking, non-religious and written in direct, concise language, this book will revolutionise your views on a variety of topics through its challenging revelations about life and the very nature of reality itself.

With its practical approach to spirituality, **Revelation** will empower you through a new awareness of the active part you play in creation and inspire you to look at your world in a whole new light.

For me, **Revelation: Joseph's Message** was my 'Aha!' moment – finally I was being presented with insights that resonated deep within my very core. My heart sang as I recognized one after the other of my own thoughts and beliefs put forth in black and white. *Joseph* is exactly what the well-beaten spiritual path needs right now and I can't wait to hear what he has to say next!
Debbie Ann Brett, **One Spirit Project – Canada.**

I don't have much time, these days, in my daily life, to read many books but once I began reading **Revelation: Joseph's Message** I couldn't put it down and read the whole book almost in one session. And I am sure that you too will enjoy exactly the same powerful experience as I did. **Revelation** will definitely change your life!
Geoffrey Keyte, **Healing International – U.K.**

---

www.josephspeaks.com

Las Comunicaciones de Josef: 1

REVELACION

Ban*d* of Light
M E D I A

English Language (ISBN: 978-1-906625-00-9)

Spanish Language (ISBN: 1-4392-5780-9)

Meeting *Joseph* through the mediumship of Michael Reccia was a privilege and felt like a reconnection with an old and trusted friend. *Joseph* speaks with a clarity, and wisdom that you will connect with at heart level. **Joseph's Message** cuts through the focus on materialism that is currently so prevalent and delivers a simple message that offers inspiration and a blueprint for both the human spirit and life on this planet. I highly recommend this book and can't wait to read the sequel.

Caroline Chaplin, **Renaissance Magazine – South Africa.**

This fresh perspective challenges us to stretch our boundaries and think even further 'outside the box'. I found some excellent information in this book, some very pertinent insights and confirmation of knowledge already acquired.

Claire Williams, **Paradigm Shift – U.K.**

www.josephspeaks.com